The ABC'S of Children's Sermons

Based on the Revised Common Lectionary Passages

Melanie J. Barton, Ed. D

WESTBOW
PRESS
A DIVISION OF THOMAS NELSON

WestBow Press books may be ordered through booksellers or by contacting:

WestBow Press
A Division of Thomas Nelson
1663 Liberty Drive
Bloomington, IN 47403
www.westbowpress.com
1-(866) 928-1240

Library of Congress Control Number: 2012917597

ISBN: 978-1-4497-6857-7 (sc)
ISBN: 978-1-4497-6858-4 (e)

Printed in the United States of America

WestBow Press rev. date: 10/24/2012

Contents

PREFACE

If you have spent any time presenting children's sermons, then you know how much energy is required. We often prepare inadequately. Many panic as the children come forward because they forgot to plan something and wonder what to share with them.

I have been telling children's sermons for over three decadcs. From my experience I am aware that adults often get as much from the lesson as the children, but we need to keep the focus on the youth. This book will help you with that process

These stories were adaptively created from my adult sermons. Each selected scriptural passage came from the Revised Common Lectionary of *The United Methodist Book of Worship* 1993 3rd edition starting on page 227. To order this text go to: www. AbingdonPress.com.

The publisher was not able to insert the CDs in this book. Order them from www.thedrmelanieshow. com. Click on the store and links tab. There are also ordering instructions at the back of the book.

INTRODUCTION

Children are quick to discern if we are just going through the motions. The content of this book is designed to be visual and auditory. There is a sample prayer at the end of each story. The seasons of the church year are clearly marked.

Look over the lectionary scriptures, the book's accompanying story, and the CD version midweek. Let some ideas form of how to present the lesson. You may choose a different scripture than the example in the book. Use whichever one you feel most comfortable presenting.

Make time to get the props suggested and add your own as desired. Share your personal experience and walk with God to make the sermonettes come alive.

The stories need to be brief, to the point, and use simple and age appropriate words. Remember children take what you say literally. Get and stay on the children's eye level. If the scripture is not read beforehand, then read it in a translation designed for their comprehension. Whether your presentation is based on the story in the book or you play the CD allow time for discussion. If the young folks remain in the sanctuary for the whole service, tailor the youth's message to the pastor's sermon. It will help them actually pay attention to it.

You may even learn something about yourself as you get in the habit of taking this task seriously. You will be blessed as you endeavor to introduce God to these children. Be prepared because the youngsters will ask questions and make comments that will inspire and surprise you. Most importantly relax and enjoy the process.

ACKNOWLEDGEMENTS

My gratitude goes out first to the children who have taught me more than I have them in the last thirty plus years. Daughter Valeria Barton reminds me to keep things in the present tense. Son, United Methodist pastor Garth Duke-Barton models the effective way to capture and keep the children's interest during the children's moment. English major and Old Testament adjunct professor daughter in-law Rebecca Duke-Barton edited the manuscript and pointed out the inconsistencies. My grandchildren listened to a few stories and let me know if they understood the point. Friend Mike Nash taught me how to use recording equipment to create the CDs. Friend Ellen Leverett, experienced children's ministry worker read the draft and suggested more positive ways to phrase things. Friend Connie Stoutamire of Keep it Simple

Photography took a variety of shots in order for me to select what fit the book best. Reverend Kaye Edwards retired Director of Family and Children's Ministries of the Christian Church (Disciples of Christ) offered helpful constructive criticism based her years of work with children's ministries. The Rev. Dr. Susan Ward Diamond pastor of Montgomery First Christian Church and current First Vice-Moderator of the Christian Church (Disciples of Christ) recommended ways to increase understanding of how to use this tool. Thanks to all of them for helping complete this thirteen-year project.

CHILDREN'S SERMONS

YEAR A

ADVENT

Sunday of Advent
Matthew 24:36-44

What are you Giving?

Items needed: a wrapped Christmas present

Show a wrapped Christmas present. Christmas is coming. It is supposed to be all about celebrating Jesus' birth. We give gifts to honor people's birthdays. What gift are you giving Jesus for Christmas? Are you making Him a birthday cake? Are you offering a prayer to say thank you for what He did for us? Are you giving presents to someone who does not get any so they will know God has remembered them? When you do these things, then you are God's messenger. What can you as a group of children do to honor Jesus' birthday? Let us briefly say some things we can do. Now let us pray about it. God please help us think of something we can do to celebrate Jesus' birthday. Amen.

Second Sunday of Advent
Romans 15:4-13

Harmony

Items needed: short piece of harmony music

Have someone play or sing a short piece of music that has voices singing in harmony. In Romans chapter 15 verse 5 it says we are to live in harmony with one another. What does that mean? When we sing harmony it means all the different voices blend together. Harmony means we are to get along with one another and accept people who are different and who may dislike us. It is hard to do. Jesus did it with the people who made fun of Him, who thought He was pretending to be someone He was not. He showed them kindness and love. The next time someone says mean things to you try showing him kindness instead of saying hurtful words back to them. Let us ask God to help us remember to do that. God next time someone says mean things to us help us remember how Jesus handled similar things and that You can help us get through it. Thanks. Amen.

Third Sunday in Advent
Isaiah 35: 1-10

God Here and There

Items needed: map of US

Show a map of the United States with a mileage scale on it. In the book of Isaiah chapter 35 verse 4 it says: "…Here is your God." How far is it from here to the next state? Point to different states and ask is God here? Is God there? How big is God? How can God be in two places at once? God is wherever we are. Discuss. God thanks for being wherever I am. Remind me of that when I feel all alone. Amen.

Fourth Sunday of Advent
Matthew 1: 18-25

Angel Visit

Before Jesus was born an angel came to Joseph, His daddy, in a dream and told him what was going to happen. Joseph was surprised. People did not often get visits from angels. Joseph did what he was told to do. He had to get things ready for the baby to be born. Most of us do not have angels come to us in dreams. If an angel came to you in a dream would you be surprised? Their job is to tell us something. Let us thank God that Joseph did what the angel told him to do and let us ask God to help us do what we are supposed to do. God when I feel like you are telling me to do something help me have the courage to do it. Thank you. Amen.

CHRISTMAS SEASON

First Sunday after Christmas
Matthew 2: 13-23

Kiss it and Make it all Better

Items needed: Band-aid for each child
What does mommy do when you fall down and hurt your knee? Does she or someone else kiss it, put a Band-aid on it, or put medicine on it? What does God do when someone hurts our feelings, or refuses to play with us, or laughs at us? Mommy can't keep us from falling down. God is with us and wants us to be safe, but He does not stop us from getting hurt. He is there to help us when we do get hurt. Next time your body or feelings get hurt ask God to give you a healing kiss like mommy does, even though it comes from a person to you instead of directly from God. God I know my body is going to have pain some time and I will get my feelings hurt. When those times come help me remember there are people that can help me feel better. Amen.

New Year
Ecclesiastes 3: 1-13

How Long is Long?

Items needed: watch with a second hand
Show a watch and have them observe the second hand as it goes around full circle in one minute. How long is one minute? How long is your favorite T.V. program? Things we like go by fast and things we think we dislike seem to go by so slowly. You may think the sermon is long and just for grown-ups, but it is for you kids too. In this worship service let us ask God to help us hear something that is interesting, that you will understand, and that you can use. God, help me hear something in church today that I understand and can use. Thank you. Amen.

Melanie J. Barton, Ed. D

Epiphany- January 6 or First Sunday in January
Matthew 2:1-12

Where is He?

Items needed: picture of newborn baby
Show picture of newborn baby

Did you ever hear people talking about a baby who was going to be born? They ask is it a boy or girl? Where will the baby be born? Have you picked out a name yet? People like to see new babies all wrinkly, crying, and needing attention. When Jesus was going to be born King Herrod was jealous. He wanted to know where Jesus was because he was afraid Jesus would grow up to become king instead of him. God protected Jesus and His parents. When you were born people wanted to see you, protect you, hold you, and to show you how much they loved you just like people did for Jesus. Let us thank God that God takes care of us. God, there are people who care about us and protect us like teachers, police workers, fire fighters, and family. Thanks for all these people. Amen.

SEASON AFTER EPIPHANY

First Sunday after Epiphany – January 7 – 13
Acts 10:34-43

Partiality

In Acts chapter 10 verse 34 it says: "God shows no partiality, but in every nation anyone who fears Him and does what is right is acceptable to Him." The word fear means here to listen to what God tells us and to do it. Another word hard to understand is partiality. Do you know what it means? It means treating some people special and others like they are worth very little. Have kids in your school or neighborhood treated you like they thought you were unimportant? Did you feel very sad inside when they did that? It hurts. Sometimes we do join in to say mean things when our friends are saying things about someone. God wants us to behave nicely toward others. We are to accept people. Can you treat people like they are important? When someone treats you badly can you still do your best to love that person? Jesus did that when people told lies about Him or hurt Him. He still was kind and nice to them. Let us try to do that and ask God to help us do it. God when people start to treat others unkindly help me to be strong and not join in with them. Thank you. Amen.

Second Sunday after Epiphany – January 14 – 20
Psalms 40:1-11
Tough Times

Items needed: a picture of a big rock

Show a picture of a big rock. Psalm 40 verses 2 and 3 say: "He drew me up from the desolate pit, out of the miry bog and set my feet upon a rock making my steps secure. He put a new song in my mouth a song of praise to our God." Have you ever gone through a really tough time feeling like you were stuck because your parents were divorcing, a parent or grandparent was dying, or you or someone you love was really sick, or someone you really care about was moving away? It is rough. We want to yell at God and say: "Stop it. It hurts too much. If You really cared about me You would stop all this bad stuff from happening." Those sad times will pass and you will have a smile on your face once again and new happy memories will be made. If you are feeling down and you want to know how to make them better, let us get your parent's permission to sit down and talk about it. God, I do not like it when bad or sad things happen that I cannot stop. When those times come help me remember to talk to you or some trusted adult about it. Amen.

Third Sunday after Epiphany –January 21-27
Matthew 4: 12-23

Fishing for Men

Items needed: fishing pole

Show a fishing pole. Jesus was walking along the shore of the Sea of Galilee and He sees two men fishing. Jesus tells them He is fishing too, but He does not have a pole or bait. So Andrew and Simon were confused. Then He tells them He is fishing for men to follow Him and to be His disciples. The brothers decide to leave their fishing business and follow Jesus. Their lives changed dramatically that day. Jesus is still looking for people to follow Him, to tell others about what He did for them. Would you like to be one of Jesus' followers? If so, you are to tell other people about Him and live your life so people will know that you belong to God. Do you want to do that? If you do, God will help you learn how. Let us ask God to do that now. God, help me live so that others will look at me and know that You and I are good buddies. Amen.

Fourth Sunday after Epiphany –January 28-February 3
Matthew 5:1-12

Bullying

Items needed: picture of some child bullying another
Show a picture of someone bullying another. The Bible says in verse 11 of Matthew 5: "blessed are you when people revile (insult) you and persecute (bully) you and utter all kinds of evil (lies) against you falsely." We hear a lot about young people who are bullied and how much that hurts the person. What do you do when someone says something about or to someone that is not true, is mean, or they bully the boy or girl? What is bullying? What can we do about it? How can we handle it? We can pray about it, tell the teacher, principal, parents, minister, get friends to back you, and if possible stand up to the bully. God when someone bullies me or someone else let me ask an adult to help stop it. Thank you. Amen.

Fifth Sunday after Epiphany – February 4-10
Mathew 5:13-20

Salty

Items needed: salt shaker

Show shaker of salt. Verse 13 of Matthew 5 says we are the salt of the earth. In Bible times salt was very valuable. People paid for things with salt. What is food like when salt is missing? It lacks flavor and is tossed aside. It is like gum that you chewed and it has no taste now. As God's children we are important like salt. We want people to look at us and see that Christians have flavor like salt, a valuable and important thing to have. Give each person a taste of a dab of salt. Describe how salt is used. Let us pray asking God to help people see how salty, how much flavor Christians have. God we want to be valuable to you and others. Please help us learn how to do that. Amen.

Sixth Sunday after Epiphany –February 11-17
I Corinthians 3:1-9

Solid Food

Items needed: a jar of baby food and baby bottle
Show the children a jar of baby food and a baby bottle. Verse 2 of I Corinthians 3 says: "I fed you with milk, not solid food, for you were not ready for solid food." How many of you remember eating baby food? It is soft, and without much flavor, or color. Babies have to have it that way until they get teeth, can chew, and their tummies can digest more solid food. When you are young in church it is helpful to have things that are easy to understand. When you are little you first learned to roll over, then to get on all fours, then to stand, and finally to walk. It is like that with understanding things about God. It comes in stages. Just keep coming and listening and asking questions, for just like a baby that is how we all grow as God's children. God, remind us it is okay to ask questions and we do not have to know everything right now. Amen.

Seventh Sunday after Epiphany – February 18-24
Matthew 5:38-48

Turn your Cheek

Matthew 5 verse 39 says if someone strikes you on the right cheek you are to turn the other cheek and not strike back. What does this mean? Are we supposed to let people beat us up? No. It means when someone does something bad to us we are supposed to show him the right way to handle things peacefully and without violence. It is hard to do that when someone is hurting us either with words or fists. The next time someone at school, in the neighborhood, or your own family says bad things to you, or tries to hurt you ask God to help you do the right thing. Handling things peacefully is different from letting people punch or hit us. Can you tell me ways you can be peaceful, but also how to keep you safe from someone wanting to hurt you? God, people are not always nice to one another. When that happens help us to think of ways to be safe and send someone for us to talk to about it. Amen.

Eighth Sunday after Epiphany – February 18-24
Matthew 6: 24-34

No Worry

Items needed: plate of healthy food, right clothing for the weather, and picture of a school

Show a plate of healthy food, proper clothing for the weather, and a picture of a school. Matthew 6 verse 25 says: "Do not worry about your life, what you will eat or what you will drink, or about your body, what you will wear." God knows what you need. Does this mean we can stay home from school, or never need to buy groceries, or our parents no longer need to go to work? No, it means we do what we can about things we can control. When we have done all we can do then it is time to trust that God will see to it that what we need, we will get, but it may be different than what we want. What things can you control? We can eat right, go to school, dress right for the weather, get enough sleep, and play out in the sunshine. When you worry about things then just sit down and talk to God like you and I are talking. Tell God what you are worried about and ask God to take away your worry. What are you worried about? God, everyone worries. I do too. When I worry help me feel You are with me and everything will be okay. Amen.

Transfiguration Sunday Last Sunday after Epiphany
Matthew 17: 1-9

Transfiguration

People hear and see things that they think may mean a certain thing, but God may want them to do or see something differently. When Peter and John went up on the mountain with Jesus they saw three figures. They saw Jesus, Moses, and Elijah. They wanted to build something so the three men could stay there, but God wanted them to do something different. People are going to tell you at times in your life: "This is what this Bible verse means for you." That may be true for that person, but God may have something different in mind for you. That is why we have to read the Bible for ourselves to see how it speaks to us. When something speaks to us we will know because a voice inside our head will tell us. That is the Holy Spirit. It is not scary, but helps us feel calm when it happens. Let us thank God that He cares about us and has things to tell us. God, help me want to read about you in the Bible. If I do not have a Bible, help me find someone who can get me one and read it to me. Have that person help me to understand about you and what you want me to do with my life. Amen.

LENT

First Sunday in Lent
Matthew 4:1-11

Shrove Tuesday

Items needed: picture of a stack of
pancakes with a picture of syrup

Show a picture of a stack of pancakes. The day before Ash Wednesday is called Shrove Tuesday, Fat Tuesday, or Pancake Day. Eating pancakes or foods high in sugar is considered a rich meal and is done the day before Lent starts. Lent is the time we remember how Jesus went into the wilderness for 40 days and went without food to get ready to do his ministry. We cannot go without eating for 40 days so we give up something that we enjoy so we can think about what Jesus did for us. Some people give up sugar or chocolate. Other people add something like reading a special book related to Lent. What can we do during Lent to prepare for celebrating Jesus' death and resurrection? Discuss and then pray. God, when I eat pancakes next time help me think about how much you love us and what Jesus did to show us that. Amen.

Second Sunday in Lent
Romans 4: 1-5, 13-17

Trouble

Items needed: picture of a pet dog

Show a picture of pet dog and tell how that dog became part of the family. Did your dog ever get into trouble, eating something he was not supposed or leaving some mess that you or your parents had to clean up? There are classes to train dogs to behave right, but it is up to the parents and teachers to train children how to behave properly. There are going to be things you do that you get into trouble. Ask God to help you to accept whatever the consequence is, but better yet, ask God to help you to think before you do something that will involve a punishment. God, when I am tempted to do something that will get me in trouble help me to think about it and choose to do something else. Amen.

Third Sunday in Lent
Romans 5:1-11

Character

Romans 5 verse 4 says endurance produces character and character produces hope. What does that mean? When a person is honest and lives the way they say they believe, then they have character. What do people say about you? Are you honest, can you be trusted, and are you kind to others? If you are, then you have good character. Having these qualities helps you have hope that good will come into your life. Discuss how it is not a guarantee that life will go well. Pray for God's help to have good character. God, I want to have good character. Please help me to learn how to do that. Amen.

Fourth Sunday in Lent
John 9:1-41

Now I See

Items needed: a blindfold for each child
Put blindfolds on each child. What can you see? How does it feel? Take them off. The man in the Bible story was blind, but Jesus made him see. Is there anything different about you that you would like Jesus to help you fix or get better? We believe God can help. Let us ask God to help you with your problem. Discuss. God, there is something I would like You to help me with. I am saying that silently in my head. Help me to notice when it gets answered. Thank you. Amen.

Fifth Sunday in Lent
Romans 8:6-11

Childhood Memories

Items needed: picture of you as a child

Show a picture of what you looked like at the age of the children listening to the story. Tell them how now you do not look like you did or act like you did when you were their age. Tell them if you still have and remember some things from that time in your life. Do you have toys from your childhood, some things you wrote, or some great memories? What symbols do you have that God is in your life? What items can the children save as they grow up to remind them about God? Maybe it is an attendance award, a New Testament when they got baptized or Bible story they like, songs you sing, Bible verses they can say, or prayers you learn. As you get older you will learn more things to help you understand God and to get closer to God. Let us thank God that we have these things. God help me find something I can save or remember to use all through my life like a prayer I say at bedtime so I can stay connected to You my whole life. Amen.

Palm Sunday

Sixth Sunday in Lent
Philippians 2:5-11

King of Israel

Today we celebrate Palm Sunday, the day that Jesus rode into Jerusalem on a donkey while the people waved palm branches and called Him King of Israel. They wanted Him to be their king and then they would get to tell people what to do. They wanted to rule the world, but Jesus served the people instead. He was a teacher, a healer, and He taught us what God is like. Did you ever want to be in charge of your parents and tell them what they had to eat, wear, when to go to bed, or tell your Sunday school teacher what you were going to do in class for the day? Jesus wanted His followers to help others and show them how to live like He did in a kind way. Today think about Jesus and how He loves you and is glad you are here in church to learn about Him and God, His Daddy. Let us pray and thank God that He loves us. Dear God, You are our heavenly Daddy. Thank you that you loved us enough that you sent Jesus to earth to teach us that. Amen.

EASTER SEASON

Easter

John 20:1-18

Plugged In

Items needed: cell phone and charger

Show a cell phone and charger. When we say that we are connected to God it means we talk to God, listen to what God says to us, and sing songs to God. If we disconnect from God in these areas, then we run out of power to do the things God wants us to do just like a cell phone's battery running out of a charge. Let us ask God help us to want to stay connected. God, each time we look at our parent's cell phones let us remember to stay plugged into You by talking to you every day just like we do with our family and friends. Amen.

Second Sunday of Easter
I Peter 1:3-9

Wise use of Time

Items needed: hourglass egg timer

Show an hourglass egg timer. Using the egg timer, ask what can you do in three minutes? It can be a long time or a short time. Sitting in time-out can be a long three minutes, playing with your friends for three more minutes until time to come inside can be a short time, playing a game on the computer when your brother is waiting to use it can be short for you and long for him. One day we will each go to be with God then all the things we did on the earth will seem like it was just a short time. Ask God to help us to do good things with our time and to cooperate when our parents tell us time is up or we have to wait longer for something. God, it is hard to be good all the time. Help us when people ask us to do things to be patient so we avoid being sent to time out. Amen.

Third Sunday of Easter
Luke 24:13-35

Getting Big

Have you ever been to a family reunion and one of your older aunts comes up to you and says, "Aren't you so and so's child? My look how much you have grown!" Then they usually squeeze your cheeks and kiss your forehead. Yuck!!! Jesus had dinner with His disciples when He came back to life after He died. At first they did not recognize Him. He looked different, but when He took the loaf of bread and broke it they recognized who He was. They got excited and were happy to see Him just like that aunt who had not seen you in a while. We can thank God that He always remembers us and loves us no matter how big or old we get. Let us pray. God, I am glad you always remember and know me. Help me not to ever forget about You. Amen.

Fourth Sunday of Easter
John 10:1-10

Wandering Off

Items needed: picture of a sheep

Show picture of sheep. Have you ever watched sheep on a farm? They all just go wherever they want unless the shepherd leads them. They want to eat grass that looks yummy so they get outside the pen and keep munching away until they are so far from the flock it is impossible to find their way back. They start bleating, "Please shepherd come bring me back. I promise I won't wander off again." The shepherd finds them and brings them back lovingly. He reminds them that although the grass looks tasty, it can lead them so far away that they are unable to find their way back on their own. Did you know we are like sheep? We get some ideas of things we want to do and wander off forgetting about church, God, and other important things. One day we notice how far we are from God and want to come back. Can we? We sure can. Ask God to bring us back to church, our family, and our friends. Remember this when you become a teenager and think church is not cool any more. God will still be here when you wander off and you get tired of trying things your way. God will welcome you back. God when I become a teenager and think church is not cool remind me that You are always there and church and talking to You is always a good thing to do no matter what age I am. Amen.

Fifth Sunday of Easter
1 Peter 2:2-10

Simple to Hard

I Peter Chapter 2 Verse 2 says "like newborn infants, long for the pure, spiritual milk, so that by it you may grow into salvation." You were born you without any teeth. You did not know how to chew food. When your mommy's milk or formula no longer satisfied you then the doctor said you could eat soft food and then meat and other chewable foods. When you first learn about God, it is just like drinking milk. We need simple things that are easy to swallow. The longer we go to church the easier it gets to understand the more difficult things about God. Just like in school you start out in kindergarten learning how to play and to write your name. By the time you graduate from high school you can often speak another language and do very hard math problems. Do you think you are old enough to learn complicated things about God? How will you know when you are ready? What is something that you have already learned about God that at first you did not understand? Let us ask God to help us understand the easy milk things and to go on and digest tough things about God. God, right now I do not understand a lot about You, but I am willing to learning. Help me always be interested in learning more about you. Amen.

Sixth Sunday of Easter
John 14: 15-21

If you Love Me

John 14:15 says: "If you love me, you will keep my commandments." What are the commandments? Go to Exodus 20 and read them. What difference does it make if we keep them? Why did God give them to us? Have you ever been at recess when the teacher was too busy to watch what has happening? What happened? Sometimes children started taking things from one another, or fighting which ended with someone getting hurt. It is just like that if we go against the commandments. We forget that God is a loving parent and wants what is best for us even if we don't want it for ourselves. The next time you think about doing something you know you are not supposed to do think about it. If God was on duty on the playground watching you, would you misbehave? Stop, think, and do the right thing. God we all do things we should not. Next time we are about to do something help us to remember You are with us and choose something that will not get us into trouble. Amen.

Ascension of the Lord
Acts 1:1-11

Reappearance

Acts chapter 1 Verse 9 says: "...as they were watching, He (Jesus) was lifted up, and a cloud took Him out of their sight." After Jesus died on the cross He came back to life and spent many days with His followers and disciples. Then when it was time for Him to leave He started to rise up off the ground and a cloud surrounded Him and He was gone. Can you imagine what that would be like? Did you ever watch a magician do magic tricks and he made an animal disappear and only to re-appear? Well, someday Jesus is to re-appear like He went. We don't know just when or how that will happen. It may or may not happen in our lifetime. If you saw Jesus coming down from the sky, what would you do? Let us ask Jesus to help us be ready for whenever that time might be. Dear Jesus, help us get excited and not scared about You coming back to earth. Amen.

Mother's Day

Seventh Sunday of Easter
John 17: 1-11

Parental Protection

What is something your mother asked you to do, but you did not want to do? What happened when you disobeyed? Did you get a spanking, restriction, or loss of privileges? Disobeying costs us something. Has mom ever had a surprise for you, but you missed it? When she called you thought she was asking you to do something, so you refused to answer so you missed out. God is like a parent to us. When Jesus was on earth He tried to protect us and help those who were confused about what decisions to make in their life. Like a parent sometimes God asks us to do things for our own good. Sometimes He asks us to avoid things that we think are good for us, but are not. God has good things for us, but at times we neglect to listen when He calls us. Let us listen to God and to our moms. God, help me listen to my parents even when I do not want to. Amen.

Pentecost

Acts 2:1-21

Like Rushing Wind

Acts chapter 2 verse 2 and 4 says: "and suddenly from heaven there came a sound like the rush of a violent wind and it filled the entire house where the (people) were sitting...they began to speak in other languages." It surprised the people who were gathered to hear talking in an unknown language and it was amazing to those who understood what they said. In some churches people speak in this way and they call it their prayer language. Sometimes it sounds like mumbling or made up words. Other times it sounds like ancient languages. When people speak in this way they say they are filled with God's spirit, called the Holy Spirit or Holy Ghost. Have you ever heard any one speak like that? People are supposed to do it if they have been given that special ability, but not brag to about it, or to say they are better than those who do not have this gift. If you ever hear someone talk in this prayer language, ask God: "are you talking to me?" Let us pray that each of us will hear God speak to us in whatever way God chooses. God, when I pray help me to believe you hear what I say and that if I get this special prayer language I will not brag about it. Amen.

SEASON AFTER PENTECOST
OR KINGDOMTIDE

First Sunday After Pentecost – Trinity Sunday
Matthew 28:16-20

Tell Them

Items needed: toothbrush and toothpaste,
a picture of a traffic light

Show tooth brush and toothpaste and picture of traffic light. Have your mom or dad told you to go brush your teeth and you whined: "I will go in a minute when I get done playing my game." If people did that at traffic lights what would happen? There would be crashes. Can you tell me what the color of the lights mean on the traffic signal? When it turns yellow we are to slow down and stop. When it is red we are to come to a complete stop. When it is green we can drive through the light. Parents tell us things to help us, even though it sounds like they are spoiling our fun sometimes. Sometimes they tell us to be cautious (like the yellow light). Other times they tell us to stop and listen (like the red light). Often they tell us to go and do something like brush our teeth (like the green light). God told us to go to tell other people about Jesus. We say wait until I am done doing this or that. We say, wait until I am older or know more about Jesus. God says go like the green light. Can you think of someone you can tell about Jesus? God, help me think of someone I can tell them about Jesus and You. Amen.

May 29 –June 4
Matthew 7:21-29

Sandcastles

Items needed: small amount of
   sandbox sand and sand toys

Build a sand castle in some sand. What happens when the water comes and washes over sand? It disappears. If we dig in dirt, instead of sand and add water, sunshine, plant food to seeds, what happens? Things grow. We are like that. We have to add good things into our lives to grow as one of God's children. Reading the Bible is our spiritual food, praying is like adding sunshine, getting baptized is like adding water to plants. You put all this together and we grow and do not wash away (do not feel all alone) when hard or bad times come. Let us thank God He gives us these things to grow. Let us remember to do them. God, thanks for giving me the things that I need to grow up knowing You are there for me. Amen.

June 5 – 11
Matthew 9:9-13, 18-26

Eating with the Rejected

When you have lunch at school who decides where you will sit? Do you sit with your friends? Is there ever anyone that is sitting off by his or her self? How come? What is it about that person that no one wants to sit beside them? Maybe they cannot afford nice clothes. Maybe they eat food that looks and smells strange to you. In our Bible passage today it tells us that Jesus made it a point to go eat with the people that others avoided. He did it to let them know God loves them. Do you think you could just one day ask to sit beside someone that no one else wants to be around? You might get teased or laughed at. Would you try it for God please? Let us pray about it. God give me the courage to go sit beside someone at school that no one else wants to. Thanks, Amen.

June 12 –18
Matthew 9:35-10:8

Dirt is Good

There once was a dog that liked to roll in the dirt after taking his bath and then come in the house and roll on the carpet. I am unsure what it is about the feel of the mud; slimy and warm that makes a dog want to do that. Do you know why they want to do that? Do you ever jump in mud puddles and then track mud in the house? What does your mom say? She tells you to wipe your feet and wash your hands. Why? God made dirt, and mud puddles and soap and water. Dirt has good things in it and it can do bad stuff too. God wants us to be clean and healthy. It is okay to play in the dirt and mud, but remember to wash off the dirt that has germs in it before we eat or track it into the house. God, sometimes we pretend that we washed our hands and face because we do not want to take the time to do it right. Help us to stop and do it right so we do not have germs on our hands that can make us sick. Amen.

June 19 – 25
Matthew 10:24-39

Numbered Hairs

Items needed: comb

Show a comb. Run it through your hair. Did you know in Matthew chapter 10 verse 30 it says: "Even the very hairs on your head are numbered." That is quite impressive. What the Bible passage is talking about today is that God knows what is going on with us and cares about us. God does not leave us all alone, but is there for us if we reach out and ask God to be there. Next time you are brushing your hair, remember that. God, I cannot imagine how You know how many hairs I have on my head. I am glad You do and want to take care of me. Thank you. Amen.

June 26 – July 2
Matthew 10:40-42

Doing Good Stuff

Items needed: cup of cold water

Matthew 10 verse 42 says: Whoever gives a cup of cold water to someone in the name of Jesus it is like giving it to Jesus. When Jesus was on the earth He was doing good stuff for people all the time. He listened to them, He healed the sick, and He accepted people who others disliked. What can we do to show God loves people? Discuss and pray. God, the next time we see someone who is thirsty like when someone is working outside remind us to get our parent's permission to take them a drink of water just like Jesus would do. Amen.

July 3 – 9
Romans 7: 15-25

Avoiding Trouble

Items needed: rubber band for each child

Show rubber bands. Pass out a rubber band to each child. Do you ever do something Mom or Dad have said not to do? Do you ever know before you do it you are going to get into trouble, but you do not care? Grown-ups are like that too. People sometimes need some special ways to help to do the right things. You can wear a rubber band. When you are tempted to do the wrong things snap the rubber band to remind you that the pain of the rubber band is less painful than the trouble you will get into if you do the thing you are not supposed to do. That does not mean to snap someone else's rubber band on their wrist. God, it is real hard not to want to snap someone with a rubber band. Help us remember to wear it for the right reason to remind us of something important like doing our homework. Amen.

July 10 – 16
Matthew 13:1-9, 18-23

We are Part of God's Garden

Items needed: picture of a garden, flower seeds
Show a picture of a garden. Have you ever helped your parent or grandparent plant a garden? Did you know we are part of God's garden? God sends people to tell us about Jesus, God, and the Holy Spirit. Some people hear the story and toss it aside. Some people hear it and really get into it and then go on to other things. Some people at first are not sure and eventually they believe that Jesus really was on the earth and died on a cross for them. Do you know that God is asking each of us to help take care of God's garden? How do we do that? We tell people the story of Jesus. Then we tell them more if they are interested. Then they too can help take care of God's garden. To be good gardeners we have to come to church to be fed stories about God and then learn how to go plant seeds (tell people about God). Give the children some flower seeds that they can take home and plant in dirt or put on a windowsill. As they grow let us remember that we are God's gardeners. God, help us to not be afraid to be Your gardeners, to tell other people about You. Amen.

July 17 – 23
Romans 8:12-25

Hope

What does hope mean? It means waiting for something that we believe is going to come. At Christmas and our birthdays we hope we will get presents. On tests at school we hope we will get a good grade. When we do something we know will get us into trouble we hope our parents or teachers will punish us lightly. It is hard to be patient for something that is exciting, but we want things that are unpleasant to get over with quickly. In today's Bible reading it talks about hoping for what we do not see and waiting for it with patience. Let us see how patient we can be listening to today's sermon before we start thinking about what we are going to eat or play after church. God, when we listen to today's sermon let us hear something that is for us. Amen.

July 24 – 30
Romans 8:26-39

Sighing

Sigh deeply. Do you know what it means when you sigh deeply? It means, if only.........if only my parents would stop nagging me to clean my room, if only I had gotten my homework done. Well, there is another kind of sighing. When we pray to God and do not know the words to say, it is like us sighing. The Holy Spirit puts words in place of our sighing and passes them on to God. Isn't that interesting? God, Sigh….. thanks Holy Spirit, for knowing what we mean to say and for telling God for us. Amen.

July 31 – August 6
Matthew 14:13-21

Feeding

Jesus really cared about people. When people came to hear Him preach and it was mealtime He took whatever food was present and stretched it to feed everyone. We are unable to perform such miracles, but we can give money and food to programs that help feed those who cannot afford to buy food for themselves. God, many children are hungry in our country help me tell some grown-up about a child I know that is hungry so they can get enough to eat. Amen.

August 7 –13
Matthew 14:22-33

Praying

Do you say a prayer before you eat or before you go to bed? Why do we pray? What would happen, if we did not? Do you know God will listen to us any time? The disciples were afraid when the waves were high. They got scared and prayed that they would be helped. Jesus came walking to them on the water. Jesus does not do that today for us, but is still there to help us in situations even though we are unable to see Him. Let us thank God for Him watching out for us. God, I get scared when I have bad dreams. Please send me a guardian angel to watch over me so I will not feel afraid or alone. Amen.

August 14 – 20
Matthew 15:21-28

Names Hurt

Words can hurt or words can heal. "Sticks and stones may break my bones, but names will never hurt me." That is untrue. Names do hurt. They last a lot longer than it takes to heal from a bruise of being hit with a stick. The woman in the story shouted out to Jesus hoping He would heal her daughter. At first Jesus ignored her request for a reason. It is what people expected Him to do since she was of a different faith, but then she spoke words that told of her faith in Him. Then He healed her daughter. Even though the crowd ridiculed her she continued to seek Jesus' healing for her daughter and believed it would work. It did. Let us not call other people names. Let us say things that are kind and helpful because they can help heal someone who is sad or hurting just like that woman in the Bible story was. God thanks that you healed that woman's daughter. Help me to say words that are helpful and not hurt others. Amen.

August 21- 27
Romans 12:1-8

Who is Most Important?

Who is most important in this church? Is it the minister who preaches the words God wants us to hear? Is it the Sunday school teacher who tells us about God and how God wants us to be connected to Him? Is it the janitor that keeps the place clean so we can worship? Is it the people who give the money so we can pay the minister, janitor, or the electric bill? Or is it you who will one day be in charge of the church? The answer is that all of us are equally important. We are the body of the church. We all have to do our parts to get it to work. What is your part? Let us say out loud some things we can do for the church. God thanks that no one is more important than someone else in church. Help me to remember that. Amen.

August 28 – September 3
Romans 12: 9-21

Living Peaceably

Live peaceably with everyone means to be non-violent. That is a pretty hard thing to do. What if someone spits in your face, or pushes you out of line at the drinking fountain? What should you do? Some people just like to see us get angry, because they believe they win when we get mad. People do not make us do things. They may coax us to try to get us to get angry or do something that is wrong. When someone does that I want you to think of it like an invitation to a party you do not want to go to. Say a quick prayer and tell yourself in your head: "I do not want to go there. God please help me remain calm and peaceful." You know what, God can do that. It may take us a few times before it works completely, but try it and you will see. God, when someone pushes me or tries to get me mad help me remember it is an invitation I can refuse. Amen.

September 4 – 10
Romans 13:8-14

Love Ourselves

Love your neighbor as yourself. What does that mean? How do we love ourselves? We do things that make us feel good, we eat things we like, and we play games we want to play. Who is our neighbor? Anyone can be. To treat people the way we want to be treated is the way Jesus lived and we are supposed to follow that. Talk about what you do when someone who is your neighbor is someone you dislike or they dislike you. How do you show love to them? God remind me to treat my family and my friends the way You would. Amen.

September 11 – 17
Romans 14:1-12

Beliefs

Some churches believe we should not eat meat and need to worship on Saturdays, the original Sabbath day celebrated in the Jewish tradition. Some churches believe we should not use glue because it is made out of horse products, or celebrate Christmas or birthdays because they believe each day should be the same and not special. Some churches believe that you have to listen to the highest authority, no matter what the person says, you must follow it. What does our church believe? What is the reason we believe that way? Which church is right? Discuss where and when your church first began. God, help me learn what our church believes and then decide what is right for me. Amen.

September 18 – 24
Philippians 1:21-30

Alive Inside

Christ is supposed to be alive inside of us. That is difficult to explain. You know how blowing bubbles feels, or how an electric blanket feels warm and soft on a cold winter's night, or how yummy hot chocolate tastes, or how good it feels to get a hug? All those experiences make us feel warm and giggly sometimes. Christ inside of you is like that. You feel warm and happy. Ask Jesus into your heart if you have not and maybe you will get the "warm all over feeling." God, I want that warm all over feeling. I invite Your Son to come live inside my heart and thank you that it is the way we get to be in the family. Amen.

September 25 – October 1
Philippians 2:1-13

The Same Mind

Do you remember the Star Trek program on television? Mr. Spock would put his fingers on someone's temples to have a mind meld with them to know what they were thinking and to connect with them. Our Bible passage this morning says we are to have the same mind in us that was in Christ. It is like a mind meld. How can we do that? We can read the things about Jesus in the Bible to see what he did, what kind of people he talked to, what he said, and how he did it. We can do that also by listening in church, in Sunday school, and the children's moment. We will learn these things so we can have the same kind of mind as Christ. Let us ask God to help us with that task. God, my mind sometimes is like mush. Help me to read things about You and to talk to You so my mind can be like Jesus'. Amen.

October 2 – 8
Matthew 21:33-46

Cornerstone

Items needed: picture of yours or some
other church's cornerstone

Show a picture of a cornerstone, yours if the building has one. Many churches have a cornerstone at one of the edges of the building. It is supposed to be strong enough to help support the weight of the building. They put things inside like a newspaper clipping about the church, the price of things in that day and time, the names of church people, etc. Jesus is our cornerstone. He holds us up, and with Him there in our lives we do not have to handle heavy problems by ourselves. He helps us. We don't have to worry about what is going on in the world, the price of food or gasoline, because Jesus never goes out of style or date. We can always count on Him. Let us say thank you to Him. God, thanks for being our cornerstone. Thanks for holding me up when I feel sad or weak. Amen.

October 9-15
Philippians 4:1-9

Are you Worried?

There is a song called "Don't Worry, be Happy." The Bible tells us we do not have to worry. Do you worry about tests at school, whether your friends will like you or not, or that your parents might get sick or divorced? The Bible passage today says not to worry about anything, but pray and give thanks to God. If you do that you are to feel calm about the things you might worry about. What are you worried about? Let us talk to God about it. God, everyone worries about something. Thanks that we can turn that over to You. Amen.

October 16-22
I Thessalonians 1:1-10

Copies

Items needed: a piece of paper with some words on it and then a Xerox copy of that original

Show a piece of paper with some words on it and a copy of that. See these pieces of paper? Can you tell which one is the original and which is the copy? There are little flecks or marks in the copy that do not show from the distance, but do when you are up close to it. We are supposed to act and be like Christ. When we do things others see us and when they get to know us they can tell whether we are acting like the real thing or are a copy that has flaws in it. Let us pray that God helps us to imitate the way Christ lived. God, help people to think of You when they see me. Amen.

October 23 – 29
Matthew 22:34-46

Close at Hand

Items needed: empty toilet paper roll and
Matthew 22:37 written on paper to go inside it
Show an empty toilet paper roll with a verse placed inside of it. I have an object in my hand that is a way to remember something important. Do you know what I have in this tube? It is a Bible passage. Can you read it? What does it say? Why would we keep something like this close at hand? It is to help us remember important things. Can you say it with me? "You shall love the Lord your God with all your heart, and with all your soul, and with all your might." Let us ask God to help us do this and remember this verse. God, I am not sure about how to love you, but will you please help me learn how to do that? Thanks, Amen.

October 30 – November 5
Matthew 23:1-12

Religious Practices

Jesus talked about people who claimed to be experts about how to do religious practices. These leaders were unable to understand that it was more important about how you acted based on what you believed rather than how you did things. The church leaders did not know who Jesus really was and what He was trying to teach them. Jesus grew up and became a minister and told people God loves them even these church leaders. God loves you even when you act like you are a "know it all." When you act like you are smarter than your friends or that you are more important than your friends, ask God to help you do things the way God would want you to. God, help me when I act like a "know it all" to remember that is not being very helpful to others. Thank you. Amen.

November 1ˢᵗ or First Sunday in November All Saints Day

Matthew 5:1-12

Saints

The Bible says that blessed are the pure in heart for they will see God. Today is the day we honor those people who did wonderful things for God that affected many people in a positive way. In the Catholic Church they actually call those people saints. Some women have seen an image of Jesus' mother Mary and because of that were able to heal people and to tell us things that Mary told them. It takes a long time for someone to be called a saint and it is often after they are already gone to heaven. That does not mean those people were perfect. We can do things that are good for God and people. If we do what we believe God is asking us to do, then we are saints in God's eyes. Let us pray that God clearly tells each one of you what you are to do to let people know God is alive and loves them. God, I do not know of any saints and I do not act like one, but thank you for those who have been saints and what they can teach us. Amen.

November 6 – 12
Matthew 25: 1-13

Come Again

Items needed: picture of a wedding

Show a picture of a wedding. There is story in the Bible passage today that talks about a wedding. People were supposed to get ready for it, but they got tired of waiting for the groom to come so they went to sleep or did other things. This story is like us waiting for Jesus to come. He is supposed to come back to earth to get us. This is called the Second Coming. No person knows when it is going to happen. We may go to heaven before it happens. We are supposed to live our lives like it could be today, not out of fear, but out of expecting something good to happen. Let us ask God to help us remember that God is going to send Jesus back and we want to be ready whenever that time comes. God, help us to live like we are ready for Your Son to come to earth at any time and to not be afraid of doing something that You would not approve of us doing. Amen.

November 13 –19
Matthew 25:14-30

Talents

God gives us things to do. It is called a talent. It may be singing, praying, collecting food for the poor, or teaching. Whatever it is when we use that skill we get better at it and God has us do additional things. If we try to ignore using that gift sometimes we no longer have it. We then miss out on how it might have helped someone or showed someone that God cares about them. If you feel like there is something special you can do let your parents, the pastor, your Sunday school teacher, or some adult in the church know so we can find a place for you to use it. You are not too young. Let us ask God to show you what you can do. God, what is my talent? Will You please help me to figure it out? Thank you. Amen.

Christ the King

November 20 –26
Matthew 25:31-46

Separating the Sheep from the Goats

Items needed: picture of sheep and goats
Show a picture of sheep and goats. Have you ever been to a farm and seen sheep and goats in one pen? They do not do well together. Sheep kind of have a mind of their own. They are like children who have trouble paying attention in school. They wander off but the shepherd always goes to bring them back. Goats are stubborn and refuse to come even when the leader calls them. The Bible says when Jesus comes back to earth the people will be separated like sheep and goats. Those who listen to God and follow Him are the sheep and the goats are those who refuse to follow God. I hope you want to be a sheep and listen to God. Let us pray and ask God to help us follow and listen what God tells us to do. God sometimes I am like a goat and sometimes like a sheep. If I forget to listen to what you tell me is the right thing to do, I ask You to speak to me in a way that I will listen. Amen.

YEAR B

ADVENT

First Sunday in Advent
I Corinthians 1:3-9

Coming

1 Corinthians chapter one verse 7 says, "…We wait for the revealing of our Lord Jesus Christ." Today is the beginning of Advent, the time we prepare for the celebration of the birth of Christ. The people that went to visit the Christ child had no idea what to expect. Never before had a poor baby been born who would grow up to become the king. We do not know what will happen in our lives as we grow up, but we hope it will be good things. We prepare to be grown up by learning and practicing things until we know how to do them. We watch and copy people who live like we want to live. As we wait to celebrate Jesus' birthday on December 25th, how are you preparing for that day? Instead of thinking, "what am I going to get for Christmas," think about what are you going to give to Jesus for Christmas? It can be a smile, a hug, tying of someone's shoelace, or taking some of your own money and buying something for a child who will not get presents. All these actions are ways we can do something for someone and it is like doing it for

God. Let us ask God what we can do for others to show God loves them. God, show us how we can be a gift to someone else who needs one. Amen.

Second Sunday in Advent
Mark 1:1-8

First Act

Have you ever watched a comedy act where a comedian is telling jokes? Before the famous person comes out another person who is not yet as well known comes and tells their jokes. In the Bible story John the Baptist started his ministry before Jesus did. It was like John was the first act getting people ready for Jesus. Jesus had John baptize Him and then Jesus went into the wilderness to prepare for the work God had for Him to do. We are preparing for the time we celebrate the birth of Christ. There will come a time that God may ask you to do something to help the world or just one person. Let us thank God that there is work for us to do and ask that we be able to recognize God's voice when it comes to us. God, when You speak to me help me to know it is really you. Amen.

Third Sunday in Advent
Isaiah 61:1-4, 8-11

Decisions

Items needed: a hand puppet

Show a puppet. Who works the puppet? The person behind or inside it does. If it has strings it is called a marionette. We are different. Unlike the puppet God does not pull strings to make us do things. We are in charge of ourselves but can ask for God's help. We can make good or bad decisions. God does not like it when we make poor choices, but God still loves us even when our decisions hurt us or other people. As you make decisions about how to behave remember God will help you, if you ask Him and allow Him to do it. God please help us to make good decisions that do not hurt us or others. Amen.

Fourth Sunday in Advent
Romans 16:25-27

Mystery

Romans chapter 16 verse 25 says, "…The mystery that was kept secret for long ages but is now disclosed through prophetic writings is made known to all the Gentiles." In the Old Testament (the books written before Jesus came to the earth) some people got messages that they were supposed to give to people about what was going to happen. One of the messages was that God would send His Son. In the beginning these secrets were only revealed to people who were Jewish because God chose those people to be His special children. The people did not want to listen or to do as God wanted them to do. The result was we people who are not Jewish were allowed to know the secrets (that God loves us and sent His Son to earth for us). We were brought into God's family. Pretty important isn't it? We don't have to keep it a secret. We can tell other people that we are getting ready to celebrate the birth of Jesus who was born on earth as God's son to let us know God loves us and wants us to be part of God's family. God thank you that we can all be Your children. Help us invite other people to be part of Your family too. Amen.

CHRISTMAS SEASON

First Sunday after Christmas
Galatians 4:4-7

God's Family

Items needed: an adoption document

Show an adoption document. In Galatians chapter 4 verse 4 it says: "God sent His Son, born of a woman, born under a law, in order to redeem those who were under the law, so that we might receive adoption as children." Last week we talked about being brought into God's family. When a family adopts a child there is often a waiting period before the final adoption papers are signed. Our waiting time was over when Jesus came to earth. He came to invite all people to be part of God's family. It does not matter where you live, what color your skin is, how smart, or how rich you are. God wants everybody to want to be part of God's family. Who do you know that does not feel like they belong anywhere? Is there someone at school who is chosen last for games, no one wants to sit by at lunch, or to be their partner? Well, Jesus would go to that person and invite them to be His friend. We can do that too. We can say to the people who make fun of others: "You know what? God loves this person and that is what I am going to do too."

Talk about those who are unlovable and how we can love them. God, thanks for adopting us. Help us remember to be kind to all people no matter what they look like or what they believe. Amen.

SEASON AFTER THE EPIPHANY

Acts 19:1-7

Baptism of the Lord (First Sunday after the Epiphany) – January 7 – 13

Accepting the Gift

Items needed: an antique item

Show some antique (or old item) you got from relatives. Tell where it came from. Ask the children if they have anything that belonged to their grandparents or other relatives. How do you take care of those items? People give us things and we are supposed to appreciate them and take good care of them. God sent Jesus as a gift to us. When Jesus went to heaven God sent someone to be with us until we go to heaven. It is called the Holy Spirit. It comes to live inside of us when we decide to believe that Jesus died for us and ask Him in. The Holy Spirit helps you to know things, to understand things, and to do what is right. When you are ready to accept what Jesus did for you and/or get baptized, the pastor or your parents will discuss it with you. God, thanks for offering baptism to us and the Holy Spirit. Help us know when we are ready to do it. Amen.

Second Sunday after the Epiphany – January 14-20
I Corinthians 6: 12-20

Temple

Items needed: picture of a temple

Show a picture of a temple. I Corinthians chapter 6 verse 19 says, "Do you know that your body is a temple of the Holy Spirit within you, which you have from God, and that you are not your own?" God made us. Our bodies are supposed to be welcoming for the Holy Spirit to be inside of us. Grown-ups and kids often do things to our bodies that over time can shut God and the Holy Spirit out. Such things are drinking alcohol to excess, taking drugs other than what doctors prescribe, smoking, overeating, not exercising, saying curse words, or doing unkind things to other people. We need to put good things into our bodies and be around people that say and do nice things. This way our body, the temple, is open for God to have us to do things like help a neighbor mow their grass, or put get someone's newspaper on their porch. Let us ask God to help us do things that are good for our bodies. God, when we eat help us think to put good food into our bodies. Amen.

Third Sunday after the Epiphany – January 21-27
Mark 1: 14-20

Following

Items needed: fishing net

Show a fish net. Jesus is starting to do His ministry. He was down by the Sea of Galilee and He saw two fishermen named Simon and Andrew put a net into the sea. Jesus told them to follow Him so they left their nets and went with Jesus. I wonder what happened to their families since someone had to work to pay for food to eat and supplies they needed. Did they tell their family good-bye or just leave? Did they go back home every so often to spend time with their family? I do not know. What I do know is they followed Jesus and it was hard on them. People did not understand what they were doing, so they beat them and put them into jail. Because the disciples kept telling the story of what Jesus had done for them today we know about it and can tell others about it. God may ask you to do something very important in your life. I want you ready to do as God asks. Let us ask God to get you ready for whatever you are to do with your life. God, when you ask me to do something help me be willing and ready. Amen.

Fourth Sunday after the Epiphany – January 28 – February 3
I Corthinians 8:1-13

Steamed up

Items needed: a mirror

Show a mirror. Breathe on the mirror. It gets all steamed up. When we get all mad or steamed up people notice us in a bad way. If we want people to know we belong to God, we need to be aware of how we are appearing to others. Discuss. God, I want people to see me as calm and helpful not all steamed up. When I get angry remind me that I can release my anger in a good way and not at a person or at myself. Amen.

Fifth Sunday after the Epiphany – February 4-10
Isaiah 40:21-31

Wait

WAIT The letters can stand for wanting answers immediately today. I want what I want when I want it. Waiting for fun things to start goes slowly. Waiting for things we do not want to do like dentist visits or shots goes fast. We are supposed to wait for God to direct our lives and He will give us strength, so we will be strong like eagles flying high. We will have the energy to continue to work until whatever gets done. If there is something we need to decide, then we need to take the time to ask God what we should do and wait for the answer. It will come. God when I am waiting for something help me remember to talk to you about it so I can be patient. Amen.

Sixth Sunday after the Epiphany–February 11 –17
Mark 1:40-45

All Kinds of People

Items needed: picture of a bathtub with water in it
Show a bathtub filled with water. Some people are unable to take a bath because they are homeless or have no water. Their body may smell. We avoid being around them. We do not like to touch things that make us feel uncomfortable. Such things are roaches, rats, dirty diapers, snakes, people who dress differently from us, or those to us who eat foods strange to us. What would Jesus say about such people? Jesus spent time with such people. It does not mean we have to become friends with all these people. We can be kind to them but avoid staring at them or talking about them. What can we do to help those kinds of people? Discuss and pray. God it is hard to be nice to people who are different from us. Help us learn how to do it. Amen.

Seventh Sunday after Epiphany – February 18 –23
Mark 2:1-12

Healing

People used to believe if you got sick it was because of something bad you did. Some friends brought a man to Jesus who was unable to walk. They wanted Jesus to make him be able to walk. Jesus told the paralyzed man: "get up take your mat and go home." The people were amazed. They never saw anyone heal a person before. Have you ever prayed that someone you care about would be healed? What if they did not get better? Was it because you prayed in a wrong way or the person did something bad? No. We just get sick sometimes. God still cares for us and loves us even if a sick person does not get better. God still wants us to pray for people no matter how it turns out. God I know someone who is sick. Would you please help them get better. Thank you. Amen.

Eighth Sunday after Epiphany – February 25 – 29
Mark 2:13-22

Chances

Jesus was down by the sea and He saw a person named Levi who collected taxes. He told the man to follow Him. Jesus went to Levi's house and had dinner there with him, other tax collectors, sinners, and His disciples. The church leaders found out and thought that was terrible. They believe He should only be around people who were like the church people. Jesus knew that people who were following the laws set up by the church already knew about God's love. People who felt no one loved them or who did bad things needed to know they could change their life and God would accept them. There are going to be chances in your life for you to hang out with people who the church would say to avoid. If you are around them to show them how God loves them, then that is good. If you decide to follow the things that these people are doing that hurt them or others, and then always remember you can come back to God and God will forgive you. God the kids our parents would say to stay away from may invite us to hang out with them. When they do help us be able to show them the right way to live. If we cannot do that help us to be strong to say no thank you when they invite us to do things that are not good for us. Amen.

Transfiguration Sunday Last Sunday after Epiphany
Mark 9:2-9

Look at my Face

Items needed: flashlight

Show a flashlight. Shine it under your chin. Look at my face without the flashlight shining on it. Now look when I shine the light on it. How does it look different? Jesus went up on top of a mountain with three of His disciples and He started to light up from the inside. God did that to Him. It was to show that God was there with Him. Do you ever feel like God is in you? Well, we can ask God to help us look like God lives inside us so other people will notice and ask about it. God when people look at me I want to live so others will be drawn to you. Please help me live that way. Amen.

Lent

First Sunday in Lent
Genesis 9: 8-17

Rainbows

Items needed: picture of a rainbow

Show a picture of a rainbow. Why does God give us such pretty rainbows? It is to remind us He will not ever cover the whole earth again with a flood. God keeps His promises, but do we? What have you promised and forgotten to keep? Did you promise to tell the truth, to help your parents, to talk respectfully, to study in school, but you forgot? Aren't you glad God does not go back on His promises? Let us ask God to help us keep our promises we make to Him and others. God next time I see a rainbow I want to remember to thank you for it. In case I do not remember I am saying thank you now. Amen.

Second Sunday in Lent
Mark 8: 31-38

Acting Right

Items needed: picture of a school desk

Show a picture of a school desk. Do you ever play school? Have you had a favorite teacher? Next time your teacher is having a bad day say something nice to him or her. Tell the children about your favorite teacher. Jesus was a teacher. Each of you is a teacher too. You teach people by the way you act. It is important to act right even when you do not know that someone maybe watching you. God we are all teachers. We teach others by the way we act. Help us to be a good teacher. Amen.

Third Sunday in Lent
Exodus 20:1-17

Ten Commandments

Items needed: tablet with the Ten
  Commandments on it

Show a tablet with the Ten Commandments on it. Can you name the Ten Commandments? Read the tablet. Which one is the hardest to follow? Covet means to want something someone else has. God wants us to have things, but not to want something that is not good for us. What is something we might want that is not good for us? Let us ask God to help us want what is good for us. God some of your commandments I do not understand. Help me know why I should follow them. Amen.

Fourth Sunday in Lent
John 3:14-21

Showing Love

Who do you love? Do you think you will always love that person? Who loves us no matter what? God and our parents do. Today show your love to someone by hugging them, helping him or her pick up a something that drops on the floor, say thank you when they give you something, or just smile when you pass by people. God show me opportunities to be helpful and to thank those who help me. Amen.

Fifth Sunday in Lent
John 12: 20-33

Believing in God

There once was a woman who said she did not believe in God. The woman's minister told her to ask God to do something to show God is real. When the minister came back to visit the woman was asked, "So what did God show you?" The woman said: "Well the only thing was in the backyard. There was this double rainbow and it was not raining." The minister said: "then your prayer was answered." She said, "I am not sure. I want more proof." It is hard for people to believe in something they are unable to see, like God. What is something that tells you God is real? Discuss and pray. God when we see a rainbow remind us that You give us that as a promise that You are real. Amen.

Palm Sunday
Philippians 2: 5-11

Love Letters

Items needed: either a green and yellow
basket or a picture of one

Show a picture of a green and yellow basket. "A tisket a tasket, a green and yellow basket. I wrote a letter to my love and on the way I dropped it, I dropped it." Did you ever write a letter to someone and got help with the spelling, if you needed it? God wrote us a love letter and we call it the Bible. There are many places in the Bible that tells us how much God loves us and wants to help us. Let us ask God to help us know that we are loved. God help me to learn Bible verses that tell us how much you love us. Amen.

EASTER SEASON

Easter

John 20:1-18

Recognition

Items needed: a picture of a tomb

Show a picture of a tomb. Mary Magdalene went to the tomb and saw the stone rolled away. People in those days buried the dead in caves. Heavy stones covered the entrance. She was unable to roll it away by herself. When she saw the stone moved and no body inside she thought someone stole His body. She was scared, but then Jesus spoke to her. She did not recognize Him at first. He looked different. When we have not seen someone in a long time they do look different, but when we get together it takes a short while for everything to be familiar and we feel okay again. There will be people in your life that are there for a while and then move away or become friends with someone else or some may die before you do. You will miss them and see them again when you go to heaven. They will change and so will you. You can ask God to help you get over missing them when they are gone. God help me to get over missing someone when they move away, become friends with someone else, or die. Amen.

Second Sunday of Easter
John 20: 19-31

Locked Door

Items needed: a picture of a door
with a bolt holding it closed

Show a door with a bolt holding it closed. The disciples were in a room locked away and scared. They thought the authorities would come take them away like they did Jesus because they had been His followers. Jesus came to them right through locked doors. He ate with them to let them know He was really alive and there was no need to be afraid. When He went to heaven He left them the Holy Spirit to be with them. We cannot see the Holy Spirit, but It lives inside of us to help us know what to do and to not feel alone. When we get scared let us remember the Holy Spirit is with us. Let us thank God for the Holy Spirit. God thank you that You sent the Holy Spirit to be with us to help us not feel alone. Amen.

Third Sunday of Easter
Luke 24:36b-48

Facing Fear

Items needed: a picture of a child showing fear
Show a picture of a child who shows a face of fear.
Have you ever felt so afraid you were unable to move?
There was a five-year old girl who lived across the street
from a cemetery. She and her sister were friends with the
caretaker. Her sister dared her to go into the building
called a mausoleum which is the place where they
buried people instead of in the ground. When she did,
the caretaker started locking the building for the night,
not knowing she was in there. She yelled, "Let me out,"
and the caretaker was afraid because he did know any
one was in there. Once out, the little girl ran all the way
home shaking. Jesus was with her when that happened,
but she was still scared. When we accept Jesus as our
Savior we are taught that He goes where we go and
feels what we feel. Now when you get scared, have a
bad dream, or feel deep sadness or pain, God is there.
Sometimes you can actually feel God's presence with
you. Have you ever felt that? You can ask for it. Let us
pray about it. God when we become afraid help us to
feel Your presence with us. Amen.

Fourth Sunday of Easter
Acts 4: 5-12

Praying for Healing

Items needed: picture of someone praying

Show a picture of someone praying. The Jewish temple rulers wanted to know by what power the disciples healed sick people. The disciples said they did it in the name of Jesus. This angered the leaders because they killed Jesus. They thought it was impossible for Him to be God's son who was sent to earth to tell us God loves us. When we pray for someone sometimes they get healed. God does the healing. When people ask you how a person got healed that you prayed for you can tell them, "God did it." People may disbelieve you just like they did the disciples. That is okay. You and I know God can and does do that. Let us pray right now for someone who is sick that we want to get better. God this person from our church is sick (fill in name[s]). Would You please make them get better? Amen.

Fifth Sunday of Easter
Acts 8:26-40

Telling

Items needed: picture of a chariot

Show a picture of a chariot. There was a man from Ethiopia who was reading the book of Isaiah in his chariot. Philip came along and saw what he was doing. He told him about Jesus. The man believed and was immediately baptized and went back to his own country. He told people about what had happened and many more people believed. There may be people who you think would not want to know about Jesus. You can still tell them and if they stop you that is okay. You never know, they might become a person who tells many others about Jesus. Let us ask God to help us overcome our fear about telling people about Jesus. God, it is scary to tell people about you. We are afraid they will laugh at us. Give us the courage to tell them anyway. Amen.

Sixth Sunday of Easter
John 15: 9-17

Showing Love

There is a song that says, "They will know we are Christians by our love." How do we show love? What things do we do? What do we do, if we are supposed to love someone, but they are not very loveable? Discuss and pray about it. God help us to show our love to other people just like Jesus did here on earth. Amen.

Seventh Sunday of Easter
John 17:6-19

Who Taught You?

Items needed: a laced up shoe, a clock, and a picture of a made-up bed

Show a picture of shoes with laces, a clock, and a made-up bed. Do you remember who taught you how to tie your shoes, tell time, and make your bed? After you watched them show you a couple of times you probably wanted to do it all by yourself, unless of course it was a chore you did not want to learn how to do. Jesus showed His disciples how to do things like take care of people who were sick, or people who needed something. Jesus only had 3 years to teach them all He could and then they had to learn the rest on their own. People here at the church try to show you how we are supposed to live like Jesus did. After a while we have to stop just watching and start doing it ourselves because people will want to learn from us. Let us ask God to help us do that. God thanks for people who teach us how to do things. Help us to do the same for others. Amen.

Day of Pentecost
Acts 2:1-21

Red

Items needed: a red stole, a red crayon, a lit candle and a heart-shaped piece of paper

Show a red stole, red crayon, fire on candles, and a heart. What do you think of when you see red? Do you think of anger, or a heart pumping blood? Red is the color we think of when the Holy Spirit entered the disciples. Ministers wear a red stole to remind us the Holy Spirit is still alive today. God when we wear red help us to remember and think of the Holy Spirit. Amen.

SEASON AFTER PENTECOST

First Sunday After Pentecost –Trinity Sunday
John 3:1-17

Fathers

Items needed: a picture of a father with children
Show a picture of a father with children. Fathers do good things for us and we do not often appreciate it until it is too late. What things do fathers do for us? We have a heavenly Father who does things for us too. What can we do to show our appreciation for our earthly fathers and for God? Discuss. God thank you for fathers and especially for You being our heavenly Father. Amen.

Melanie J. Barton, Ed. D

May 29 – June 4
Mark 2:23-3:6

You are not Supposed to Do It

Items needed: either grain samples
or picture of heads of grain

Show a picture of grain. Jesus and His disciples were walking through a field of grain. Jesus stopped and plucked some heads of grain. The disciples said. "You are not supposed to do that on the Sabbath (the day they worshiped God)." People were supposed to not cook, to only walk so far, to not work, and follow many other rules. Jesus was trying to teach them that there is a place for rules and a time that rules need to be put aside. What if there was a rule that said you could only come to this church if you had a lot of money? What if there was a rule that said no one by the name of Smith could take communion? These are silly rules. When rules are made there is a good reason. It protects people from bad and hurtful things. There are times that rules no longer apply. For instance, it used to be against the law to buy toilet paper on Sundays because it was considered unnecessary. There used to be "blue laws" that said stores had to be closed on Sundays. That is no longer true. What rules do you have in your house? What is the reason for the rules? When you get older you will get to make some rules. Think carefully the reason you are making them and change them when they no longer fit the situation. God we may not like the rules, but when we get old enough to make some remind us to be kind to those who are supposed to obey them. Amen.

June 5 –11
I Samuel 8:4-20 (11:14-15)

Kings

Items needed: picture of a king

Show a picture of a king. The people in the Old Testament refused to listen to what God instructed them to do. Samuel was appointed by God to be the judge over the people, but he was getting old and people wanted something different than have a judge over them. They wanted a king like the other nearby nations. God allowed them to have the king, but they still were unhappy. Even then they did not want to do what God asked them to do. How often are we like that? We say to our parents, "if you will buy me that new game, I promise I will behave for a whole month." Parents give in and we break our promise. God wants us to do things that are suggested to make our lives better so we can feel happier and life can be less troubling. Let us ask God to help us follow the things God would like us to do. Discuss. God we want to be in charge. Help us to follow Your suggestions and to keep our promises. Amen.

June 12 –18
Mark 4:26-34

Growing

Items needed: a picture of a garden

Show a picture of a garden. Have you ever planted a garden? Did you start with seeds or a tiny stalk of a plant? If you measured the plant before you go to bed and again in the morning, you may find it has grown bigger during the night. You have to water it and give it enough sunshine, rain, and get rid of the weeds around it so it can grow. We are like a garden. We need water (the Bible to hear about God's plan for us), we need sunshine (God's light to shine through us), and we need to get rid of the weeds in our life (the bad habits like talking back to our parents). Tell me some other ways that we are like a garden. God thanks for giving us the Bible to read to help us grow up knowing about you. If I get some bad habits in my life that are like weeds help me get rid of them. Amen.

June 19 –25
I Samuel 17: (1a, 4-11, 19-23) 32-49

Just a Boy

Items needed: show a picture
representing David and Goliath

Show a picture of David and Goliath. This is the story of David and Goliath. Goliath was a big bully who scared everyone. He was threatening the people of Israel to a challenge, to kill him or be killed. David was just a boy but he believed he could take care of the situation. It does not say he was not scared. It says he just solved the problem. He put a stone in his slingshot and flung it at the giant hitting him in the forehead and killing him. Have you ever been asked to do something that was meant for someone much older than you to handle- like someone getting hurt and you had to call 911? You will have times in your life that you are asked to do something and you will think: "I am not old enough, smart enough, or strong enough." When those times come for you to do some important task ask God to guide you to do the right thing. God when someone asks us to do something and we do not feel old enough or stronger enough remind us we can ask You for help. Amen.

June 26 – July 2
Mark 5:21-43

Weaving Together

Items needed: a piece of embroidery with threads knotted and tied on the backside

Show the backside of a piece of embroidery. Explain that the tapestry has threads of all colors, shapes, some tied, and some broken. It is like our lives. God makes us into a beautiful piece of work, but sometimes we have to go in a different direction, become a different color of thread (married, single, sick, well, move, go through loss of someone) to produce the completion of who we are at the end of our lives. Use the color of threads to represent different events (green for the color of a graduation gown, white for a wedding, black for a death, red for love, etc.). God thank you that You have a plan for our lives. Amen.

July 3 – July 9
II Corinthians 12:2-10

People who Heal

Items needed: a medicine bottle
   with the label still on it

Show a bottle of medicine. Who in your family has to take medicine? Do you, your parents, or grandparents have some condition like allergies, diabetes, heart problems, or something else? Some people say you just have to believe in God and God will make you all better. God allowed people to create pills to help people get better. God also uses doctors, nurses, therapists, friends, and teachers to help us with our problems and illnesses. Some people take things when they should not. Some people take more than they should. We need to ask God to help us take the right things when we need to take medicines and to see the right people to help us heal. Who do we need to pray for that needs help or to get better? Have children pray out loud for those people. God hear the names of the people mentioned and please help them get better. Thank you. Amen.

July 10–16
II Samuel 6:1-5, 12b-19

Showing Thankfulness

Items needed: simple musical instruments
for the children to use

Show a person dancing and a tambourine or harp.
King David was a man who liked to dance when he
was happy. The people used all kinds of instruments.
They played lyres, harps, tambourines, castanets,
and symbols while they sang. This was their way of
saying thank you to God for the good God had done
for them. How do we show our thankfulness to God
in our church? Do we have a praise band or musical
instruments in church? Each person worships God in
his or her own way. Some are very quiet and private.
Some are loud and dance and sing songs that make
them feel good. Which way is most comfortable
for you? It does not matter which way you praise
God, it only matters that you do. Let us take these
instruments now and make a joyful noise unto the
Lord. Dance around the sanctuary and then come
back. God please accept our music we played for
You as a way we show we love You. Amen.

July 17- 23
Mark 6:30-34, 53-56

Sheep

Items needed: picture of a sheep

Show a picture of a sheep. A sheep wanders away from the flock just lazily eating the grass wherever it takes him. Suddenly he looks up and is lost from the herd. He bleats (the sound sheep make), hoping the shepherd can hear and come find him. We are like that. We do things that are harmful to us. We wander away from doing good, going to church, start hanging around kids who say bad words, or unkind things about other kids. Before you know it we are so far out there we cannot see our way back. We can always ask God to come find us and help us get back into the right herd of people, get back into church, and listen to the minister who is our shepherd, and to our Sunday school teachers who tell us how to live right. Let us ask God to remind us of that when we are tempted to get too far away from God and the church. God when we start to wander away from church and do the things that separate us from You please invite us back. Amen.

July 24 –30
II Samuel 11:1-15

It is Mine

Items needed: picture of two
children tugging on a toy

Show two children tugging on a toy. Have you ever watched two year olds playing? When they see something they want they say, "It's mine, all mine." They do not want to share. They do not want you to take it away from them. If it was ever theirs to them it is always theirs. They want what they want when they want it and if they do not get it they throw a tantrum. Some people in the Bible were like that. King David was. He wanted things that did not belong to him. We people are like that too. When people take things that do not belong to them, it affects them. They end up paying for it in one way or another. They feel guilty, or get caught and have to go to jail, or pay a price, or someone gets mad at them. When you want something that you know belongs to someone else what should you do? God we think about doing or taking something that does not belong to us help us stop and not do it. Amen

July 31 – August 6
John 6:24-35

Making Bread

Items needed: flour, yeast, salt, sugar, water,
a baking pan, and a loaf of spelt wheat
bread from a health food store

Show all the ingredients to make bread. Spelt is a kind of wheat that has been around since Bible times. Show a loaf of it (find in health food store). God gives us the ingredients to make this food that is good for us. He makes the sunshine and the rain to make the grain grow. He gives us eggs to use to hold the bread together. The salt and the yeast give it flavor and make it rise. God thank you that we have been given all these ingredients to make good food to help us to grow up to be strong and healthy boys and girls. Amen.

August 7 – 13
Ephesians 4:25-5:2

Releasing Anger

Items needed: A non-latex balloons

Blow up the balloon slowly. Say to the children: "See how the hot air can be used for good to make it get big?" If you get mad it is like having a lot of hot air. We puff up inside our bodies and we get a feeling of pressure in our chest. If we let the air out quickly it makes a sound and can blow the air onto someone. That is like letting our hot anger out on someone. It does not feel good to have that happen to you. If you instead use that hot air to let it out in an appropriate way not directed at any person we can be seen as a good person. So let us stand up and pretend we have hot air and blow it toward the center of the circle. Can you feel the temperature? Now just let the air out slowly and feel your chest slowly go down. That feels better. So when you get mad think of how that feels in your body and how it can hurt other people. God help us let go of our anger in the right way. Amen.

August 14 – 20
John 6:51-58

Communion

Items needed: communion cup with grape juice in it, communion bread

Show a picture of the communion elements. Today's Bible reading talks about eating the flesh of Jesus and drinking His blood. Are we cannibals? No we are not. What is it talking about? It is about communion. Some churches believe when you take communion the bread actually becomes the body of Christ and the grape juice is actually Jesus' blood even though you cannot see it. Some churches believe that the spirit of Christ enters into the bread and cup but it still remains the bread and cup. Some churches believe it is just an exercise to remember what Christ did. What does your church believe? What are you supposed to do to get ready to take communion? What are you supposed to be thinking about while you take communion? Discuss. God when I am old enough and ready to take communion help me understand what it all means and to take it seriously. Amen.

August 21 – 27
Ephesians 6:10-20

Whole Armor

Items needed: a picture of armor
with the various parts visible

Show a picture of armor. God asks us to put on the whole armor of God. The parts are: a belt, breastplate, shoes, shield, helmet, and sword. The belt goes around our waist to remind us to tell the truth. A breastplate of righteousness reminds us to be pleasing to God. Shoes are to make us ready to tell the world about Jesus. A shield of faith is to represent our belief in God. A helmet of salvation stands for us being saved by Jesus. The sword of the Lord means to be able to stand up to whoever tries to attack our belief in God. In your life there are going to be times you will feel all alone and that no one understands you. Other times there will be people trying to get you to be angry or will tease you about your beliefs. To prepare for difficult times picture putting on this armor as a protection. Then listen in church to know the truth of what God has done and will do for us. Be honest and not make up stuff. Be ready to tell people about Jesus when they feel all alone or scared. No matter what happens to you, God is always with you giving you the strength and courage to face whatever comes your way. God is our armor. God help me feel strong and have courage to face whatever comes to me. Amen.

August 28 – September 3
Mark 7:1-8, 14-15, 21-23

Washing

Items needed: washcloth and toothbrush

Show a washcloth and a toothbrush. Why do we wash our hands before we eat? Why do we brush our teeth and wash our face? What if your mom and dad were more interested in whether you washed with Ivory soap than whether you got clean, or that you that you had to wash your hands for exactly three minutes to get clean enough? Would that make you mad? It would me. During Bible times some church leaders were more concerned about how long, and how often you did things, and whether you did them exactly as instructed rather than just doing them. If you failed to follow their rules, then they said it did not count to please or worship God. Jesus told them they missed what mattered. We are going to ask God to help us remember what is important –that we come to church and do our best to live the way Jesus showed us. It is unimportant if we have fancy clothes or if we sing praise hymns or old hymns. It is important that we come to worship God and to hear what the sermons say that can help us learn more about God. God help me to listen to the sermon and learn something and not worry about what people are singing or wearing. Amen.

September 4 – 10
Mark 7:24-37

Healing Different Times and Different Ways

Jesus had the gift of healing. In today's world some people have the gift too. It is God working through them to help people get better. At times the healing is slow like a person going to the doctor and taking medicines to get better. It may happen when a person talks to a therapist that helps him or her work through their problems. Sometimes people are prayed for and they get better immediately. We do not know why all people do not get better. Jesus told His disciples that they would be able to do what he did. You can be a healer too. It might be through talking to someone, praying for them, growing up to be a minister, doctor, or therapist. God how do You want me to help people? Please show me. Amen.

September 11 –17
James 3:1-12

Tongue of Fire

Items needed: a picture of a tongue with a flame coming out of it to represent the Holy Spirit

Show a picture of a tongue that has a flame coming out of it. Our tongue is a fire. Out of our mouths come some pretty hurtful, stinging words that lash out at people like fire would do. When we say things without thinking people can feel sad or have it feel like you punched them in the stomach. Because of what you said or did then they can then feel like they are not loved, or any good. Once you say something mean about someone or to someone you cannot take it back, but you can ask for forgiveness. God help us to stop and think before we speak to engage our minds before our mouths. Amen.

September 18 – 24
James 3:13-4:3, 7-8a

Wise People

Items needed: either a picture
of an owl or a toy one

Show a picture of an owl. The wise men looked for Jesus when he was born. Other people go find wise people to answer their questions. The owl is a symbol of wisdom. Who is wise in your house? How did they get that way? You are wise because you are in church listening to what God has to tell you. Be an owl. Listen and see what wisdom God has for you today. God help me to listen in church today to find out something new about You. Amen.

September 25 – October 1
James 5:13-20

Respectable

Items needed: a picture of hands folded in prayer

Show a picture of hands folded in prayer. The prayer of a respectable person is powerful and effective. How old do you have to be to pray about something? Do you have to know the person to pray for them? God wants us to pray about people and things. When we do that and see prayers get answered. That helps us believe more that God is real and is with us. Who do we need to pray for today? Have the children do sentence prayers for each of those concerns. God hear the prayers of each child today. Amen.

October 2 – 8
Mark 10:2-16

Getting Married

Items needed: either a picture of a bride
and groom or small figures of them

Show a picture of a bride and groom. Are you going to get married when you grow up? What will your husband or wife be like? How many years will you be married? Will you ever fight? Will you make up? God wants us to get into a marriage (permanent relationship with someone we love and that loves us), to stay in that relationship, but sometimes that does not happen. Let us ask God to pray for the person that you will spend your life with that the person will be doing what they are supposed to be doing so when you meet you will recognize each other. God I am praying right now for the person I will one day marry. Help me be ready when that person comes into my life. Amen.

October 9-15
Mark 10:17-31

Following

A man asked Jesus, "What do I have to do to be a follower of yours?" Jesus told him, but the man was unwilling to do it. He liked his possessions and that was the one thing he was not willing to give up. Now days we don't have to live in fear that someone will arrest us if we are Christians and go to church. In some countries people do get threatened and sometimes hurt or they will go to jail, if they do not worship God the way that ruler of the country says you must. If it were risky to come to church, do you think your parents would still bring you? Maybe they would leave you at home because they would not want to risk you getting hurt or them going to jail and there would be no one to take care of you. Let us be thankful that we can come to church without being threatened and without being told how to worship. God thanks that we can come to church and not be afraid of others hurting us. Please help those people be safe in countries where it is risky to go to worship You. Amen.

October 16-22
Hebrews 5:1-10

Priestly Robe

Items needed: a ministerial robe

Show robe. Why do ministers wear robes? In Old Testament Bible times when a priest was appointed it was very important event. They wore special robes, anointed him with oil, and put the blood of a ram on his right ear, the thumb of their right hand, and the big toe of their right foot. He wore a robe of blue cloth with golden bells and purple and scarlet pomegranates on the hem. This robe was to show that the priest was different than the other people, completely dedicated to God's work. Today many ministers wear robes for the same reason, but not as fancy. You might be called some day to be a minister yourself. We all need to act like we are wearing clothes that say we belong to God and are trying to tell other people what God can do to help them in their lives. God no matter what we wear let us act like we belong to You. Amen.

October 23 – 29

Mark 10:46-52

Answered Prayers

Items needed: write this title on a piece of paper or a notebook: *My Answered Prayers*

Show the picture or notebook. When people ask God to heal them of their illness or problems what do they do when the prayer is answered? Do they say the doctor healed me or my problem just went away? When we ask for something when we pray and we get the answer, we need to tell people that our prayer was answered. It is a good idea to write down the things you pray for and the date you prayed. Write down when it was answered and how it was solved. Go back and look at your list later. Sometimes the answer is different from what we asked for, but it was answered. Give the children a form that they can write the requests on and ask them to bring them back in a certain length of time to review. This is a good tool for the whole congregation to use. God thanks that You answer prayers. Help me to remember to write down my requests and answers so I will not forget that You do hear our prayers. Amen.

October 30-November 5th
Mark 12:28-34

Questions

The church authorities were trying to trick Jesus by having him answer their questions in a certain way. Jesus knew what they were doing and handled the situation correctly. It frustrated the church leaders because they misunderstood that Jesus really was the Messiah, the Savior of the world. They thought he was just stirring up trouble. There are going to be times in your life that as a follower of God people will ask you questions trying to trip you up. Things like: "why does it say in the Bible an eye for an eye, (meaning if someone hurts you then you can do the same to them), and in another place it says: do not kill?" These are questions that grown-ups can help you answer. When those troubled times come ask for God's help to know how to answer those questions. You can always say: "I do not know the answer, but I will take you to my minister and maybe my pastor will know." Let us ask God to help us when those times come. God sometimes it is hard to be Your follower. Help me to ask for help when those times come. Amen.

All Saints or November 1st

John 11:32-44

Falling down and getting back up

Items needed: a pair of roller skates

Show roller skates. Who taught you how to ride a bike or roller skate? When you fell down or wobbled when you tried to steer did you see your parent's face? It was one of worry and fear that something bad would happen to you. Sometimes that is how we learn things, by falling down and getting up again. I believe that God loves us like a parent and sometimes we have to learn things the hard way. It may be difficult for God to be with us, watch us go through things, and not interfere. Let us thank God that we have parents that teach us things and for God allowing us to try things for ourselves. God thanks for my parents and thank you that You are my parent too. Amen.

November 6 – 12
Ruth 3:1-5, 4:13-17
Taking Care of Older Folks

There was a woman whose husband died. Normally a woman in Bible times would go back to her family she grew up in if her spouse died. Ruth did not do that. She stayed with her mother-in-law who had no sons or family to take care of her. As we get older we need people to help take care of us. The way we treat people when we are well is the way they will treat us when we get sick and old. Let us be nice to people as if God were right there beside us. When we do this we will feel better inside even if the person we are nice to is grumpy. Talk about any aging relatives they have. God I have this grumpy relative. Help me to have patience with that person like You do. Amen.

November 13-19
I Samuel 1:4-20

Promises

Items needed: a picture of a rainbow
and cross your fingers

Show a picture of a rainbow and fingers crossed.
The rainbow is a promise from God. When we cross our fingers behind our back it means we do not really mean what we are promising. When we make promises we need to keep them like God does. When we give our hearts to Jesus He promises us it belongs to Him and He will keep our hearts. Discuss. God rainbows are Your promise to us that You will not flood the whole earth again. Thanks for keeping your promise. Help us to keep ours. Amen.

November 20-26

John 18:33-37

Monkey in the Middle

Items needed: a big soft ball

We are going to play the game Monkey in the Middle. Someone gets on each end and one person is in the middle. The people on the end toss a ball over the head of the person in the middle. The person in the middle tries to catch the ball. If that person is successful then they go to the end and the person who threw the ball goes into the middle. Sometimes as kids we get caught in the middle of arguments between parents especially if parents are divorced and we go back and forth to visit them. When someone tries to put you in the middle of an argument tell them, "my minister says I am not supposed to be in the middle. If you have a problem with that, talk to God about it, but don't take it out on me." If your parent gets mad about you saying that, then call your pastor. Discuss. God people will try to get me to take sides in an argument. When that happens remind me that I do not have to take sides and let the people figure out their situation without involving me. Amen.

YEAR C

ADVENT

First Sunday in Advent
I Thessalonians 3:9-13
Direction

Items needed: a picture of a conductor
directing an orchestra

Show a picture of a conductor directing an orchestra.
I Thessalonians chapter 3 verse 11 says, "Now may
our God and Father Himself and our Lord Jesus direct
our way to you." What does it mean to direct? Make
motion like an orchestra conductor, like a policeman
directing traffic with a whistle, or show a GPS getting
directions to come to the church. This is saying that
God is supposed to direct us. Where to? To get us to
be in conversation with God, to ask God what God
wants us to do, and to listen for the answers. Being
here in church is where we learn to do that by others
showing us and by the minister telling us what God
has told that preacher to tell us. Listen while I ask God
to direct you. God please help us to listen to your
direction for our lives. Amen.

Second Sunday in Advent
Luke 3:1-6

He's Coming

Items needed: an advent wreath

Show a picture of an advent wreath. Do you know what Advent means? It is the coming or arrival of an important person. Who: Jesus. It means the time we celebrate leading up to the date of Jesus' birth, the four Sundays prior to December 25th. How are you getting ready for Jesus not Christmas? Would you like to make a card and sing Happy Birthday to Him on Christmas? Discuss when and where to make. God thank you for Jesus being born. I hope our card will show how much we love Jesus. Amen.

Third Sunday of Advent
Philippians 4:4-7
Supplication

Philippians chapter 4 verse 7 says, "Do not worry about anything, but in everything by prayer and supplication with thanksgiving let your requests be made known to God." What do you think supplication means? It means the person who is praying is asking God for something either for themselves or someone else. What do you worry about? Have you tried praying about it? Ask each person to say one thing they worry about and then pray specifically for that concern. God please hear our worries and please help us to believe that You will take care of the worry. Thanks, Amen.

Fourth Sunday of Advent
Luke 1:39-45

Believing

Items needed: a picture of a man with a dog

Show a picture of a man with a dog. Did anyone ever tell you something and that you thought was untrue? There was this minister who had a dog. The neighbor told the preacher that his dog was sick. Because the neighbor lied so much the pastor did not believe her, but she was telling the truth. (Tell your own example of something someone told you that you did not believe, but it was true). When your mom or dad or grandparents tell you something, listen even if you are unable to see or believe what they are telling you. In today's Bible scripture it talks about a prophet named Micah who preached what God told him to, but the people did not want to believe it. Read about it in Micah 5:2-5a. God help us believe the truth when we hear it. Amen.

CHRISTMAS SEASON

CHRISTMAS SEASON

First Sunday after Christmas Day
Luke 2:41-52

Getting Lost

Jesus went with His parents to a festival. All the relatives got together. When it was time to leave, Jesus' parents thought He was in the group somewhere with the relatives. They traveled a whole day before they discovered He was missing. Mary and Joseph went back to Jerusalem and found Him in the temple asking questions and listening to the teachers. His parents must have been scared and mad. Have you ever not gone with your parents when they were leaving some place and all of a sudden you realize they are gone? It is scary. If that ever happens to you, do you and your parents have a plan about what to do? God wants us to be safe. We need to let our parents know where we are and where we are going. Our parents also need to tell you, if they are going somewhere different than where they said they would be. Discuss. God if we ever get separated from our parents help us to know we will be all right and to know what to do. Thanks. Amen.

SEASON AFTER THE EPIPHANY

First Sunday after Epiphany Baptism of the Lord –January 7-13
Acts 8: 14-17

Coming to Church

Did you know there are some things you can get out of coming to church? Like what, you ask? You can get some good friends who show you how to live like God wants us to do. You can hear some important stories about God and Jesus and Jesus' disciples. You can learn about some things that can hurt you and other people such as lying, stealing, and saying bad words. What can you do to get the most out of coming to worship? Ask the children for some answers (get enough sleep, eat a good breakfast, not argue with family, put a smile on your face, come expecting to hear something that will be interesting). Discuss. God help me get a good breakfast and good night's sleep before I come to church so I can listen and learn things that are helpful for me. Amen.

Second Sunday after Epiphany – January 14-20
John 2:1-11

Being Different

If you do things differently from most people someone might say you are a geek or weird, a person that should be avoided. Jesus did things differently and people misunderstood him. They wanted to be around when He did miracles that helped them. When He did things that made people think about how they treated each other, or how they did not help someone they got angry. You may want to do things that others may say make you weird or a geek. They may say that because it might be different from what they would do or they might not have thought of it first. If you get a good idea that you are afraid others will think is crazy, talk to God about it or someone you trust. Then go for it. God maybe some of the things I do other people think are weird, but help me to know if they are the right things for me to do. Thank you. Amen.

Third Sunday after Epiphany – January 21-27
Luke 4:14-21

Reputation

Verse 14 of Luke chapter 4 says, "Jesus filled with the power of the Spirit,....returned to Galilee and a report about Him spread through all the surrounding countries. He began to teach in their synagogues and was praised by everyone." Did you know that people watch what we do and say? They often report to others what they think we are like. We want people to see us do good things so they will say we have a good reputation. We want people to know we are connected to God so they will like what they see and want to have that same relationship with God. How can we show good behavior? Discuss. God help me to have good behavior that others will notice and want to be connected to You like I am. Amen.

Fourth Sunday after Epiphany – January 28-February 3

Jeremiah 1:4-10

Kids Can do

Items needed: a picture of a truck on a bridge
Show a truck on a bridge. Kids can do great things that even grown-ups can't do. There was a truck stuck on a bridge. It was too tall so it would not fit under the steel supports. All the adults scratched their heads trying to figure out how to solve the problem. Then a child said, "Why don't you let all the air out of the tires and push the truck across?" They did and it worked. Jeremiah was only a kid when God called him. God can ask you to do things. How can you know if God is asking you to do something? Discuss. God if you ask me to do something help me to know it is really You. Amen.

Fifth Sunday after Epiphany –February 4 –10
Luke 5: 1-11

Trusting

Items needed: a picture of a fishing boat

Show a picture of a fishing boat. When Simon Peter was fishing Jesus came along and said, "Put your fishing nets in the deep water." The men had fished all night and caught nothing, but Jesus said to do it. Simon Peter did and he got so many fish that his net was breaking so others had to help haul in the catch. Have you ever watched the program "Deadliest Catch"? Men go out in the freezing cold weather to get crabs. There are times when they get no catch and other times it is overflowing. In your life there will be times you are told to do something by a parent, teacher, or safe adult that your parents trust. You may not understand the reason for doing what they say, but you will eventually understand. I am telling you today, I want you to read your Bible regularly. There are important things in there that will help you when your life seems like there are no fish coming into your net or you feel like you are all alone out in an ocean somewhere. God will You help us understand what the Bible says and help us to listen when trusted people tell us things for our own good. Amen.

Sixth Sunday after Epiphany –February 11-17
Luke 6:17-26

Blessed are the Hungry

Items needed: a bag of M and Ms without peanuts *Have a bag of M and Ms without peanuts.* Give each child a handful of m and ms (get parental approval first). Tell them to hold them. Watch what they do. Do some sneak them into their mouths or pockets? Ask them what it felt like to want them and not be able to eat them? Blessed are the hungry for they shall be filled. Do you ever get filled up on enough m and ms? Are you hungry to know God and what God wants you to learn? Once you begin studying the Bible, you are supposed to get hungry for more just like when you eat a few m and ms or Lays potato chips. God help us to get hungry to find out what the Bible has to tell us that can help us in your life today. Amen.

Seventh Sunday after Epiphany – February 18-24
Luke 6:27-38

Peaceful

Items needed: green ribbons for each child

Have green ribbons one for each child. Pass out a ribbon to each child. Do you know why I am wearing this green ribbon? It means I want the earth to be healthy and the people peaceful. I want poor people to have what they need. I want the earth to be safe and unpolluted. I want people to be treated fairly. Do you know anyone who is poor? What could you do to help them not be so poor? Do you know any place that has a lot of trash lying around? Could you help recycle some soda pop cans, or plastic to help our earth be less polluted? Do you know someone who gets picked on at school? Could you maybe for one day treat them kindly and see what happens? These are things that God asks us to do to help the earth be healthy and peaceful. Can you help me do that? How? Discuss. God help us think of ways to make the earth be healthy and peaceful. Amen.

Eighth Sunday after Epiphany – February 25-29
Luke 6:39-49

Logs and Specks

Items needed: a small log

Show log and point to your eye. Jesus asked the people, "Why do you see the speck in your neighbor's eye, but do not notice the log in your own?" We are very quick to point out what is wrong with someone or what they are doing wrong. We forget to look at ourselves and see what needs to be corrected in our own life. The next time someone tells you what is wrong with you, think about it, pray about it, and notice that the person judging you probably has his or her own faults, but keep them to yourself. Pray for them. Sometimes if you become their friend you will find out they were really jealous of you. Give an example from your own life. God when someone tells me that something is wrong with me help me listen and ask You if it is something I need to work on. Amen.

Transfiguration Sunday Last Sunday after Epiphany
Luke 9: 28-36

Transformers

Items needed: a transformer toy

Show a Transformer toy. This power Transformer changes into other things. We are like a transformer when we allow God to change us. We become a new person. Old bad habits go away and new good habits begin. God transform us into something good and useful to You. Amen.

LENT

First Sunday in Lent
Luke 4:1-13

All Alone

Did you ever get separated from the kids you were with and get scared? Did you start to cry because you thought they left you on purpose? Did someone help you find them? Are there times you feel like you are lost or all alone? Everyone does. God when those times come let me feel You with me God and to not be afraid. Amen.

Second Sunday in Lent
Luke 13: 31-35

Would you go?

Jesus is healing the sick and casting out bad things inside of people. The church leaders come and tell Him to leave. If He stays the government will kill Him. Jesus leaves because it is not the time yet for Him to die. What would you do if you were in a place doing work for God and someone told you that you had to leave? Would you go? Discuss. God when I do things for You people may not like it. Help me know what to do when those times come. Amen.

Third Sunday in Lent
Luke 13:1-9

Figs

Items needed: a package of Fig Newton cookies *Show package of cookies and pass one to each child but checking for allergies.* Do you know what kind of fruit this is? It is a fig. Do you know what it tastes like? Try a bite. It is sticky and sweet. Have you ever had a fig Newton cookie? They are made from figs. Figs grow on trees (show a picture of a fig tree). It is a kind of fruit that has been around a long time. Jesus had figs when he was a boy. Can we pretend we are eating it with Jesus now? Listen, as the Bible is read this morning because it talks about figs. Next time you eat a fig Newton think about Jesus eating the same fruit when he was your age. Jesus it is fun to eat what you ate. Help us to grow up to learn to be more like you. Amen.

Fourth Sunday in Lent
Psalms 32

Sin

What is sin? Is hitting someone for no reason sin? How about if you hit someone who hit you first? Is cheating on a test a sin? How about thinking about cheating on a test? It depends on what you do with the thought. Discuss. God sometimes we do things that we know are wrong like hitting someone. When those times come help us ask to be forgiven and tell the person we are sorry. Thank you. Amen.

Fifth Sunday in Lent
John 12: 1-8

Smelly

Items needed: perfume, aftershave items to smell
Show perfume and aftershave samples to smell. Why all the smelly stuff? Years ago there was no inside plumbing and no water heater to heat bath water so people did not bathe as often. They would put perfumes on to take away the body odor. I don't think it worked, do you? Why do we want to smell good? God looks on inside and sees that. Have God on the inside and will have a good outside. God thanks for inside plumbing and heated water. The next time we have to take a bath and do not want to help us be thankful that we have water and heat. Amen

Sixth Sunday in Lent/Palm Sunday
Philippians 2:5-11

Emptying the Trash

Items needed: a trashcan

Show the trashcan. Who empties the trash at your house? Every household has their own way of doing it. In some houses the dad does it or the kids do. Just because people do things differently it does not mean that their way is wrong. All of us have trash inside of us, things like bad thoughts about other people. God can empty out the trash inside of us just like we do the recycle bin on our computer. Talk about it. God help us to empty out the trash that is inside of us like bad thoughts about other people. Amen.

EASTER SEASON

Easter Sunday
John 20:1-18

Hide and Seek

Do you like to play Hide and Go Seek? Children hide while someone counts to 100 by 5s and then the counter says, "Ready or not, here I come." Sometimes the hiders are in plain sight, but we do not see them. When Mary went to the tomb she was looking for a dead body, not a living, breathing once dead human. That must have been scary. You are going to have situations in your life as you grow up where you miss something that was in plain site. Let us ask God to help us be aware of what is going on and if you need help finding something, ask God to send you someone who can help you. God when I cannot see things that are right in front of me open my eyes so I can. Thank you. Amen.

Second Sunday of Easter
John 20:19-31

Knowing God

Items needed: a television

Show television. What is your favorite television program? What if you could see the actors in person? Wouldn't that be exciting? People want to see and know God. Meeting God can be more exciting than television. God please send me people who can help me get to know You and show me what You are like. Amen.

Third Sunday of Easter
John 21: 1-19

Life Preserver

Items needed: a picture of a life
preserver on a cruise ship

Show a picture of a life preserver and people on a cruise ship. What are the purpose of lifeboats and life preservers? When things get too bumpy and life is too scary remember you are on God's boat and with Him holding you up. It is like a life preserver and you will be okay. God when things in my life are stressful and I get scared let me feel You right there with me calming me down. Amen.

Fourth Sunday after Easter
John 10:22-30

Porches

Items needed: a picture of a house with a porch

Show a picture of a house with a porch. Does your house have a porch? Years ago porches were popular. Kids sat on a porch swing and thought about what they would do when they grew up. They watched their neighbors come and go and talked to people as they walked by. Our Bible reading this morning talks about Jesus walking under the porch of Solomon. I wonder what He was thinking about and to whom He was talking? Listen to the story when the Bible is read. God help us to live the way You want us to. Amen.

Fifth Sunday of Easter
Acts 11:1-18

Listening

Items needed: a bed pillow.

Put head on pillow and then ask. Did you ever have a dream that came true? Did you ever get the feeling God wanted you to do something? The scripture passage this morning talks about Peter having a dream to go meet with a person that he thought he was supposed to avoid. If you take time to listen, God may say something to you in your head that you are supposed to do – a good thing not a bad thing. Then you can pray about it and ask God to make sure that is what you are to do. Then go do it. There was a man who was told to go buy a gallon of milk and take it to a certain house. It was in a neighborhood he was scared to enter. The thought kept repeating in his head. Finally, he just went and did it. When he knocked on the door he felt silly. What would he say to explain him standing there? As soon as the door opened a woman shrieked. He thought because she was afraid, but it was for a different reason. She did that because her baby needed milk and she prayed and asked God to send some and God did.

Listen because God may ask you to do something for someone. Discuss how to know if it is God's voice. God if you ask us to do something help us to know how to tell if it is really You talking to us. Amen

Sixth Sunday of Easter
Acts 16: 9-15

Purple Cloth

Items needed: purple cloth

Have sample for them to see and touch. Jesus came back to life after he died on the cross. After a while He left and went to heaven. He sent the Holy Spirit to people when He left. Those people were so excited about it that they wanted to tell others about God and what happened to them. One woman who did that was a businesswoman. She sold purple cloth. It was very expensive due to the dye used to make it. Only the rich could afford to purchase it. Lydia heard Paul speak about Jesus down at the river. She believed what she heard and invited Paul and the other men to come stay at her house. She got so excited about learning about what Jesus did she started a church service in her home. Do you get that excited when telling someone else about Jesus or what God has done for you? God help see all the good things You do for us and help us to want to tell others. Amen.

Seventh Sunday of Easter
John 17:20-26

If You Love Someone Show It

When you love someone you are not afraid to tell people about it. Jesus knew God, His father loved Him and Jesus told the people on the earth that God loved them too. If you love someone you show it by doing things for them, saying nice things about them to others, and spending time with them. Do you love God? How can you show it? Discuss. God we want to show You that we love you. Thanks that You love us. Amen.

Day of Pentecost
Acts 2:1-21

We are all Different

Items needed: people of all races and countries in different outfits

Show a picture of people in diverse outfits with different skin colors. Have you ever been in an airport and you see people with all different skin colors, different clothes, and talking in other languages? It seems strange to us just as we do to them. Back in the early days after Jesus went to heaven the disciples were in a room and the Holy Spirit came. Each disciple began to speak in languages they did not know. The people gathered there spoke in these different languages and they were amazed that they could understand what was being said. That is the day we say the church began. Today people may dress, look, talk, and worship different from us, but we are all God's children and God loves all of us. Next time you hear a person speak in a different language say to yourself, "God loves that person and me. Thank you God." God thanks that You made us each different from one another. Help us learn from each other. Amen.

SEASON AFTER PENTECOST

First Sunday after Pentecost –Trinity Sunday
Romans 5:1-5

First Words

The first word some babies say is Da Da. What was your first word? Today we honor fathers. Today be grateful for God our heavenly Father. What do fathers do? They teach, love, punish, wait, cry, and push bikes. God does some of those things too. Do something nice today for your dad and for God. God please accept this prayer as our way of telling You we love You and are glad that You are our heavenly Father. Amen

May 29 – June 4
I Kings 18:20-39

Secrets

There is this song the band named the Beatles sang called "Do you want to know a secret?" The song says, "Listen do you want to know a secret? I'm in love with you." It is no secret that God is in love with us. When we listen to what God tells us we feel that love. Prophets tried to tell the people what God expected from them, but they did not want to listen. So listen for God to talk to you when you say your prayers, sing songs in church, or hear the Bible read. You will hear how much God loves you and will be able to show it to others. God help me hear You when You tell me You love me. Amen.

June 5 – 11
Luke 7:11-17

Making it all Better

Items needed: Medicine bottle for cuts

Show medicine bottle. Did Mommy or Daddy ever kiss a booboo and put medicine on it to make it all better? Sometimes people try to help us when we are sad. It is like putting medicine on our sadness. God can help us get over being sad. God when we feel hurt, or sad, or mad please send somebody to help it go away. Thank you. Amen.

June 12 – 18
Luke 7: 36-8:3

Smelling Good

Items needed: a jar of pleasant smelling ointment
Show a tube or jar of something that smells good.
A woman brought some ointment to rub on Jesus'
feet. This was to show how much she believed He
was God's son. Do we do things to show others that
we love God? How can we do that? Discuss. God
help us think of ways to show others that we love
You. Amen.

June 19 – 25
Luke 8: 26-39

Showing to Others

Some people do not believe in God and want proof that God is real. Some people believe that following people who do bad things is more exciting. Those people are the ones who sell drugs, hurt men, women, and children, and steal things from others. Did you know that you and I are the people who are supposed to show those who are looking for God that God is in us? Sometimes the way we show that is to do something to help someone such as: fix a broken bike, take food to the sick, or help a family get to the grocery store when their car is broken. The people who want to follow bad leaders also look at us. They think they can control us and make us do bad things like them. God please send Jesus into our hearts, so can be part of Your family which will make it easier to follow the examples set by good people. Amen.

June 26-July 2
Galatians 5:1, 13-25

Loving

Galatians chapter 5 verse 14 says, "Love your neighbor as yourself." How do we love ourselves? Do we hug our own body? Do we say in the mirror, "I love you?" Who is our neighbor? Is it the person beside you in church, school, or your neighborhood? What about our neighboring countries? What if the person is not very loveable? Discuss. God some people are not very loveable and sometimes I do not feel very loving to myself. Help me to learn to love myself and others like You do. Amen.

July 3 – 9
Galatians 6: (1-6) 7-16

Doing what's Right

Do you ever get mad watching kids who do things wrong like cheat on tests, have their parents do their homework, or who take other kid's things? It is even worse when they never seem to be caught. It makes you wonder if you should do like they do, because it looks like fun. Verse 9 in our reading today tells us to not give up in doing what is right, as it will eventually pay off. God when we see someone do such things will You help me see that doing right is the best thing to do in the long run. Amen.

July 10 – 16
Luke 10:25-37

Helping

Have you ever seen kids pick on someone at school? Have you watched someone beat up someone who was smaller, weaker than the bully? The story in the Bible passage is about a man who got beat up and was left on the side of the road. Some people passed by and did nothing to help the man. Finally, someone who was unrelated to the man's family or religion stopped and helped and took him to a place and paid for him to get well. What is the reason we do not help people when we see they are in trouble? Are we afraid the bully will hurt us too? Discuss what you can do about such situations. God give us courage and wisdom to know what to do to help. Amen.

July 17-23
Colossians 1:15-28

Baptism

Items needed: baptismal tank or font

Show where baptisms are done. When we first decide that we are going to follow Jesus we sometimes are excited. When we get baptized and come up out of the water (or sprinkled) we feel clean and ready to go forward. Sometimes after awhile when we are teenagers or in our 20's we think church is boring and has nothing for us. Later when we have kids we decide we need to go back and get involved again. You are here because someone loves you and wants you to learn about God and have a personal relationship with God. There may be times that you do not want to come to church. You would rather do other things, but remember God is here and is waiting for us to come and learn more about Him and how God can help us in our life. If you get bored, tell the minister so things can become exciting and helpful. God when church seems to be boring to me help me find exciting things I can learn and do. Amen.

July 24 – 30
Luke 11:1-13

Grace

Do you say a prayer at meal times? Do you think about the words? "God is great, God is good. Let us thank Him for our food. By His hands we all are fed. Give us Lord our daily bread. Amen." Does God give us our food? Farmers plant it, weed it, and harvest it when it is ripe, but God provides the rain and sunshine to make it. Discuss. God thank you for farmers and for sending rain and sunshine to make our food grow. Amen.

July 31 – August 6
Luke 12: 13-21

Being Rich

People think if you make a lot of money you will be happy. They have done shows on television about people who have won the lottery and how miserable they were. It did not solve their problems or make them happy. If we remember to keep God in our life and ask what we are supposed to do with our life, it will not matter how much money we make. We will feel good about ourselves, like what we do, and be happy. You can give money to God now from your allowance or from the money your parents give you to buy games. That way you will feel a part of God's work. God please help us figure out what we are supposed to do and be when we grow up. Amen.

August 7 –13
Hebrews 11:1-3, 8-16

Going on a Trip

Items needed: a suitcase

Show a suitcase. Did you ever go on a trip with your parents and they would not tell you where you were going? They said just pack. Abraham was told by God to pack up and go. He did because he trusted God to guide him. You are going to have things happen in your life that will make you wonder, where am I going, what is going to happen to me? When that time comes talk to an older person, the minister, or your parent to learn from their experience how to handle things. Be sure to talk to God about it too. God help us to remember to ask for help when those times of not knowing where we going or what will happen. Amen.

August 14 – 20
Hebrews 11:29-12:2

Winning the Race

Items needed: a picture of people running in a race
Show a picture of people running in a race. Have you ever won a race? How did you do it? You probably kept your eyes on the finish line. Being a follower of Christ is like running a race. We are to keep our eyes focused on God and what we can learn to make our journey/run better. Let us picture that we are in a race. Close your eyes. Now see the finish line and picture Jesus waiting for us at the end. God thank you for helping us to stay on this path in life. Amen.

August 21 – 27
Jeremiah 1:4-10

Hearing the Call

When you are outside playing and mom calls you in for supper, do you ever pretend you are deaf to her voice so you can play longer? We each are called to do work for God. We can pretend we are deaf to the call, or that we are too busy, but God will get through to us no matter how hard we try to avoid Him. Often it may come while you are just about to wake up or go to sleep. You will hear this voice inside your head that tells you things you know is right. Do not be scared; God is not going to ask you to do something bad, and you won't have a horrible life by following God. God help us open up our ears to hear when we are called and help us to answer. Pray.

August 28 – September 3
Luke 14:1, 7-14

The Right Reason

Why do we do things for other people? Is it because we want to or we think if we do we will get something in return? If we do something nice for our parents or teacher, do we think that maybe when I mess up they will not punish me, or my teacher will avoid embarrassing me when my test results are lower than others? Jesus wants us to do things for people for the right reason. Jesus helped men and women who others thought He should stay away from because they had different beliefs and practices. Jesus wanted all people to know that God loves them and accepts them. Next time you see a person who feels left out; think about what you can do to help them know that God loves them. God help us to show people you love them. Amen.

September 4 – 10
Philemon 1-21

Praying

I remember you in my prayers. Have you ever heard someone say that? What is the reason someone would do that? Do you think praying makes a difference? Ask the children to give examples of prayers they prayed that got answered. Give examples of people on the prayer list that the church prayed for and got better. Ask, "Whom do we need to pray for today?" God please hear our prayers and answer them. Amen.

September 11 – 17
I Timothy 1: 12-17

Afraid

Items needed: a picture of the
World Trade Center Towers

Show a picture of the World Trade Center Towers. This week is the anniversary of the attacks on the World Trade Center Towers September 11, 2001. Our government is working so nothing happens like that again. If you get scared, or have a question, you can ask your parents, or pastor, or someone else you trust. God hears our prayers and will help us to be brave. Let us remember the people who died on that day and the people who helped with the rescue and got sick too. God we thank you for policemen, firemen, military, and our government who all help us in many ways. Amen.

September 18 – 24
I Timothy 2: 1-7

King on the Mountain

Have you ever played King on the Mountain? The way you win is to push off the person that is on the top of the hill. Rulers around the world want to prove that their country is the greatest and the most important one in the world. Some of the leaders of those countries tell people how they must live, worship God, how much money they can make, and what they can and cannot say about their government. Our country was founded because the people wanted to worship God without the government telling them how they must do it. Prayer is still offered today at the beginning of each session in Congress. They make our laws. It is good that they ask for God to guide them. On our money it says "In God we trust." It is important for us to continue to ask God how we are supposed to live and to protect the rights to say what we need to say, work where we want to, and how we can worship. God thank You that we can worship as we want to. Amen.

September 25 – October 1
I Timothy 6:6-19

Money

Items needed: dollar bill

Show a dollar bill. The love of money is the root of all kinds of evil. What kinds of evil can having money get us into? Does this mean it is bad to be rich? If you hurt others to get money, that is being evil. If you take things away from others and lie about doing that, then that is a kind of evil. Having money is okay. It is how you act about it. If you give a proper amount of your income to God that is good, but if you hurt others and do not care, that is bad. If you practice handling money correctly then later you will be able to handle larger amounts of money appropriately. How many of you have a savings account? How many of you get an allowance? How many of you give something to Sunday school or church out of your own money? God help us handle money as we are supposed to no matter how much we have. Amen.

October 2 – 8
I Timothy 1:1-14

Praying for People

Did you know before you were born someone was praying for you? They prayed that you would be healthy; that the delivery would be safe, and that your mom would be okay too. Since then there have been other times people prayed for you and others in your family. You are never too young to pray for others. Why don't you write down on a piece of paper (get help with spelling if you need to) people you want to pray for? Put the date that you made the list and then go back and look at it a week later. Write down when and how the prayers were answered. Being a regular praying person is a great responsibility that I believe you can handle. God help us know that our prayers do matter. Thanks that we can talk to You this way. Amen.

October 9 –15
Luke 17:11-19

Staying Away

Some people who had a skin disease approached Jesus when he was on his way to Jerusalem. Because it was thought that the disease was contagious they were supposed to stay away from other people. When Jesus approached them they asked Him from a safe distance to have mercy on them. They did not directly ask that they be healed. He did something unusual. He told them to go to the priest. You see, only the priest could declare such people cured, so they believed and went as they were told and showed themselves to the priest. Their skin disease was gone. Only one of the 10 healed people said thank you for what Jesus did. Do we remember to say thank you to God for what God does and has done for us? God does things like provide us with enough food to eat, clothes to wear, a house with a livable temperature, and a workable car to go where we need to go. Let us not expect those things to just happen. God thank You that we have what we need. Amen.

October 16 – 22
II Tim 3:14-4:5

Timothy

Do you want to be a Timothy? What is it? It is a person who is called to be a minister from his home church. How do you think God tells people they are going to be a minister? What would you do if you heard a voice inside of you telling you that you were chosen? Every person has work they can do for God. Let us pray that you will be willing to do what God asks. God help me know what I am supposed to do and help me be willing to say yes when You tell me. Amen.

October 23 – 29
Joel 2:23-32

Locusts

Items needed: a grasshopper

Show a grasshopper. Grasshoppers are cousins to locust. Locusts have been around since the Bible times. They like to eat green things and come in droves. People would spend time praying, fasting, blowing trumpets, and wearing special bracelets to keep them away. Magicians even tried making special stones. One time in Utah the locusts started coming to eat the crops in the field. Then sea gulls came out of the sky and ate up the locusts. Sea gulls are now the state bird in Utah. That is strange because sea gulls do not live in Utah. People in other countries consider locust to be a delicacy to eat. They eat them raw, roasted, cooked, dried, crushed, ground, or put into dishes with bread or mixed with honey or dates. Locusts are supposed to be good for us to eat, but they can destroy a lot in a short time. God allowed them to do damage. God also provided that they are nutritional to eat. I do not want to eat a locust even if it is chocolate-covered. Other things can destroy us like hurtful words, misusing our environment, or getting angry with people who are different from us. God help us be kind to Your earth and people. Amen.

October 30 – November 5
Luke 19:1-10

Seeing

Items needed: a picture of a parade

Show a picture of a parade. Did you ever go to a parade and someone was blocking your view? You try to look around them, through them, over them, under them, but you cannot see. You can ask that person to please move so you can see too. When we do things that are hurtful to others, we block their eyes from seeing God. We are supposed to be like God and live like God would want us to do. If you are doing something that is not showing a good example, ask God to help you change that. God help us to change something that is blocking people from seeing You through us. Amen.

All Saints or first Sunday in November
Ephesians 1:11-23

Inheriting

Items needed: an antique family heirloom item
Show an antique. Do you have something that used to belong to your parent, or grandparent, or other relative? It is called inheriting something. Many times the item is not worth very much money, but it means something special to us, because it is all we have left of our loved one. When we believe that Jesus died for us we get to live with Him in heaven after we die. Because Jesus is in heaven getting ready for us He has someone here on the earth to help us until we go there. It is called the Holy Spirit. You cannot see it, or touch it, but it is there like the wind blowing through our hair on a windy day. God thank you for the gift of the Holy Spirit and that Jesus is getting a place ready for us. Amen.

November 6 –12
II Thessalonians 2:1-5, 13-17

God sees the Good

Sometimes when we do things for the church and God we get tired. It can be discouraging when we do not see anything good happening, no new people coming to church, or no new people serving in church positions. We wonder why we are doing this. This Bible passage says, "May God comfort our hearts and strengthen them in every good work and word." God sees the good we try to do and appreciates it. God when we get discouraged please remind us that the good work we are doing does matter. Amen.

November 13 – 19

II Thessalonians 3:6-13

Pretending

There are some people who pretend to love God, but their actions do not show it. They may gossip about other people, or say curse words, or say or do hurtful things to people. God tells us we are to stay away from that kind of person. If you know someone in this church, at school, or in your neighborhood that is hurting you or someone else, please tell your parent, your teacher, or your minister. God if we know someone is hurting someone else give us the courage to speak up and send us the right person to tell it to. Amen.

November 20-26
Luke 23: 33-43

Going Somewhere

Items needed: a travel brochure

Show the travel brochure

Do you like to visit different places? People get advertisements in the mail each week wanting them to go visit some place. We never get an advertisement in the mail showing us what heaven will be like and inviting us to go there. I wonder what an ad would look like. Would it have angels singing, streets of gold, and a picture of St. Peter at the front gate? I do not know. I want to go there, and when I do I am sure it will be beautiful, more beautiful than any place I have ever seen. Do you want to go there when you die (not now!)? If you do, tell God you do and that you believe Jesus died and paid the ticket price for you to get in there. Discuss. God thanks that we get to go to heaven. Thanks for Jesus paying for my ticket. Amen.

About the Author

The Rev. Dr. Melanie J. Barton is a holistic psychotherapist. She has a Master's degree in Social Work and a Doctorate in Pastoral Counseling. Dr. Barton is a licensed independent social worker and a member of the National Association of Social Workers. She is an ordained Christian Church (Disciples of Christ) minister. Dr. Barton has been telling children's sermons for over three decades. She has an Internet international radio show called *The Dr. Melanie Show* on the Health and Wellness channel of Voiceamerica. com. It airs Thursdays at 1pm EST www.voiceamerica. com/show/1929/the-dr-melanie-show. Her website is: www.thedrmelanieshow.com. She has published poetry, a magazine article "Who gets the Church when Couples Divorce", on-line articles about eating disorders, closing a therapy practice abruptly due to a medical crisis, and her life story. She currently lives in Tallahassee Florida with her multigenerational family.

Review

THE ABC'S OF CHILDRENS' SERMONS FROM THE REVISED COMMON LECTIONARY by Dr. Melanie Barton is a book that should be in every pastor's and church storyteller's library. Whether you use the Common Lectionary or not, this is an invaluable resource for weekly Children's Sermons. Easy to use, well written, theologically sound, and with an accompanying CD to overhear each week's sermon, you will want to use this resource regularly to help children learn the stories of God in a creative and imaginative way.

Dr. Susan Ward Diamond
Senior Minister
First Christian Church (Disciples of Christ)
1705 Taylor Road
Montgomery, AL 36117

To Order the CDs for *THE ABC'S OF CHILDRENS'*
SERMONS BASED ON THE
REVISED COMMON LECTIONARY PASSAGES

Go to: www.thedrmelanieshow.com

Click the store and links tab and then on the following banner

THE ABC'S OF CHILDREN'S SERMONS BASED ON THE
REVISED COMMON LECTIONARY PASSAGES
CDs

To Comment about this Book

Contact: Melanie J. Barton, Ed.D

drmelaniebarton@gmail.com

Printed in Great Britain
by Amazon